WALK
OF THE
WEEK 2

WALK OF THE WEEK 2

Peter Evans

Illustrated by
Glen McBeth

MERCAT PRESS
EDINBURGH
www.mercatpress.com

First published in 2005 by
Mercat Press Ltd.
10 Coates Crescent
Edinburgh EH3 7AL
www.mercatpress.com

Design
Iain Donnachie, www.iaindonnachie.co.uk
and Angus Bremner

Cover design
Glen McBeth and Iain Donnachie

ISBN: 1841830917

Printed and bound in Great Britain by
Bell & Bain Ltd

The walks originally appeared in *Scotland on Sunday* and are reproduced by
permission of Scotsman Publications Ltd.

CONTENTS

INTRODUCTION

WE are fortunate in Britain in having such a wide variety of scenery, celebrated liberally by artists and writers down the years, many of whom loved to visit the wilder corners of our country and capture their essence on canvas or in word. It really is a walker's paradise that can be enjoyed in every season, as long as the appropriate skills and experience are acquired.

As a proportion of the country as a whole, Scotland has more wild scenery than anywhere else, with only 10 per cent of the UK's population, so people are few and the landscape expansive. Walking north of the Border can be a very different experience for those who are used to the gentler terrain of the south.

There's the distinction of Ben Nevis as the highest peak of course, at 4,406ft; but it's not the only one rising above the 4,000ft contour and there are four more to be found in the Cairngorm massif, now contained in a national park. Move down a notch, and the mountains above 3,000ft, and below them those above 2,000ft,

will keep you occupied for years. That's quite apart from the beautiful, wide open straths and glens and the less demanding but no less interesting rural countryside at more moderate levels.

This little book is packed with a wealth of opportunity. It follows an earlier companion volume also containing 52 walks that appeared in *Scotland on Sunday*. Walkers snapped it up and clearly welcomed having the collection drawn together in a book. The response encouraged illustrator Glen McBeth and myself, with the backing of Mercat Press, our publishers, to compile another selection – all different from the first – providing a total of 104 walks from which to choose.

Natives of Scotland and visitors alike will have their own special corners regarded with particular affection, to be visited and revisited time and time again. Living where I do in the Clackmannanshire town of Dollar, I'm fortunate to have the Ochils on my doorstep. Rising 2,000ft above the flat Carse of Stirling, stretching to the River Forth, their folds and gulleys have

provided me with endless pleasure as I've got to know them over the past 18 years. But my wanderings have taken me much further afield, too, into virtually every corner of the magnificent Scottish landscape. I hope, through the pages of this book and the first volume, to share some of my enthusiasm with you, aided by Glen's distinctive illustrations. They bring the history and folklore connected with these walks to life, adding to the obvious attractions of scenery and wildlife. The history gives us influences from the early Celtic tribes to the Romans, and territorial clashes between the Scots and the English with scenes of bloody conflict.

■ If there is one thing certain about the weather in Scotland, it is uncertainty. There are gloriously sunny days, very wet and very cold ones. It is prudent to go equipped for changing conditions, particularly on higher level outings into the mountains, and to listen carefully to weather forecasts before setting out. While walks descriptions

are as accurate as they can be, changes on the ground may be encountered through land management activities and forestry operations. In the main, however, there should be few problems providing you exercise common sense. The directions offer a good general guide, but the relevant Ordnance Survey or other maps should be carried, together with a compass and the ability to use it, especially in wilder terrain.

■ The red deer stag stalking season takes place from July 1 to October 20. Recorded phone messages on some estates allow walkers to avoid sensitive areas. Further information is available on www.hillphones.info.

■ The routes range from easy strolls to much more demanding treks up Munros – designated peaks over 3,000ft. In winter they will often demand mountaineering skills, with the need to carry an ice-axe and crampons, but in summer should not be beyond the capability of any reasonably fit walker.
Peter Evans

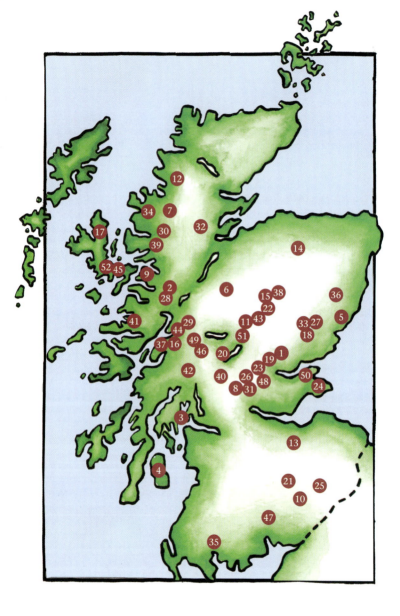

LOCATIONS

LOCH OF THE LOWES

Ospreys are magnificent birds, and we are fortunate in Scotland that they are doing well. One place to see them is from the hide at the Loch of the Lowes visitor centre.

THEMES Osprey nests are always a target for unscrupulous egg thieves, and like all raptors they have also been the subject of persecution on some estates by over-zealous gamekeepers.

To see one fishing in the wild is not such an uncommon experience these days. Luck is a factor of course, but patience and a little research about where to look will pay dividends. The sight is dramatic as the bird swoops on its prey and lifts it clear of the water. To be virtually certain of seeing one – at least during the nesting season – visit one of the RSPB reserves at Loch Garten, near Aviemore, or Loch of the Lowes in Perthshire, where there are well-established nesting sites and the birds can be viewed through binoculars and telescopes and on webcams trained on the nests. Both reserves are worth the visit anyway, as a great family day out with lots for children to see and do. This walk adds some healthy exercise to a Loch of the Lowes visit. Starting from Dunkeld gives it the bonus of readily available refreshments on return at the end.

ROUTE From the main car park in Dunkeld turn right along the main street in the direction of the bridge over the Tay and look for Brae Street on the left.

Follow this uphill at first, then it levels out. At the sign for Haughend, turn left along a track up through mature woodland. Go through a gate and in about 200 yards leave the track for a path on the left. Follow this to meet another track at a gate. Carry on to meet a minor road and go left along this to the car park entrance for Loch of the Lowes. After visiting the reserve, return to the gate where you joined the road and walk back along the track to a fork where you should turn right towards Fungarth. Go through a gate past South Fungarth and at the next sharp right-hand bend keep straight ahead through gates to reach the edge of Dunkeld and Birnam golf course. Take the track going sharply back and up to the right. Follow it through the golf club car park and on to the A923. Cross the road, go up steps and on towards a wall with a plantation beyond. Turn left through beech trees to join a track through the plantation. Turn left at a path junction, through a gate and into open woodland. A broad main track is reached. Go left down to meet the A923, then right to follow the road into Dunkeld.

Loch of the Lowes

Fungarth

Dunkeld

A9

MAP	OS Sheet 52, Pitlochry to Crieff
DISTANCE	5 miles (8 km)
RATING	Easy. Mostly tracks and paths
GEAR	Boots and a waterproof

FIVE SISTERS OF KINTAIL

Some mountains beg to be photographed, and if you scan postcard selections in any tourist haunt, along with the likes of Buachaille Etive Mor, Suilven and Ben Nevis, you are likely to see views of these shapely maidens.

THEMES Irresistible to the lenses of the landscape paparazzi, these glamorous females are a bit like the five sisters in Jane Austen's *Pride and Prejudice*. They must be approached with due respect and sensibility if you go courting them, but a day spent in their company will prove pleasurable indeed. The Bennets of *Pride and Prejudice* had no connection with the Jacobites, of course, unlike our delectable Kintail quintet. The walk starts at the Glen Shiel battle site, where a ragged Spanish force, that had suffered losses sailing to Scotland, was routed by Hanoverian troops. Hence the name of the mountain above, Sgurr nan Spainteach – Peak of the Spaniards. Two cars are needed for this walk, unless you can arrange a lift from the Loch Duich end. The owner of the Kintail Lodge Hotel once obligingly drove my companion and I up the glen. There are no worries about stalking restrictions, because the ridge is in the ownership of the National Trust for Scotland. Autumn is a wonderful time to catch the colours in this area, but start early and watch your navigation if it's misty.

ROUTE From Glenshiel Bridge, climb the steep and unrelenting slopes alongside the forestry plantation, making for the ridge above. It is best to stay right, following the burn near the forest boundary. Aim for the dip between Sgurr nan Spainteach and Sgurr na Ciste Dubh. Once on the ridge, and after a much-needed breather, turn left for the summit of Sgurr na Ciste Dubh, the first Munro of a superb day's ridge walking. A large cairn marks the top, and a wonderful view is on offer across Coire Dhomain to Sgurr Fhuaran, with its eastern ridge thrusting towards lonely Glen Lichd. Some work is needed to get there, so descend from Ciste Dubh and turn north for the next top, Sgurr na Carnach, then down into a dip above Coire Dhomain to the right. It's a short, steep climb of 600ft to the summit of Munro number two, Sgurr Fhuaran, and its cairn perched on a narrow table at 3,505ft. Push on north for Sgurr nan Saighead – an exposed and dramatic top. Loch Duich lies ahead, below the ridge, and the walk can be completed by descending Sgurr nan Saighead's west ridge to finish south of the Kintail Lodge Hotel, or by continuing over Sgurr na Moraich to meet the eastern extremity of Loch Duich.

Sgurr na Moraich   Sgurr nan Saighead   Sgurr Fhuaran   Sgurr na Carnach   Sgurr na Ciste Duibhe

Glenshiel Bridge

Kintail Lodge

Loch Duich

MAP	OS Sheet 33, Loch Alsh and Glen Shiel
DISTANCE	10 miles (16 km)
RATING	Strenuous. Rough mountain paths
GEAR	Full hill-walking kit

BISHOP'S SEAT

Not a high hill, but it will test your mettle as you tackle heather and wet moorland to win panoramic views across Dunoon and the Firth of Clyde.

THEMES A bit of rough is sometimes good for the soul – and no, we're not talking matters of a sexual nature here but of the hill-walking kind. Hardy seekers after outdoor adventure will know exactly what I mean. These are walks that forsake the beaten track for Mother Nature in the raw, and if you want to get down and dirty, there's no better opportunity than a climb up Bishop's Seat on Argyll's lovely Cowal Peninsula. Legend has it that a local clergyman climbed Bishop's Seat every day and said a prayer. All I can say is, I hope he had a good breakfast first, because although it barely breaks the 1,500ft contour, this is no hill for wimps. Much of the ground around it comprises peat, sphagnum moss and heather, so it's not terrain for the faint-hearted. But the rewards are there in the wildlife and especially those amazing views out over Dunoon and the Firth of Clyde towards Bute and beyond.

ROUTE From the east bay area of the town, make your way along John Street on to a forestry track that bears right behind houses. It angles gently upwards through trees to a track junction. Turn left along another track, gradually gaining height. Continue for around one and a half miles to a point where two successive paths appear on the left, leading back down into Bishop's Glen. Just after the second of these, leave the forestry track on the right and follow a rough path up through a ride in the forest. The path is boggy in places and there are small ditches to cross, but anyone reasonably fit will cope. Persevere until the top edge of the plantation is reached. The summit of Eilligan lies above. Ascend this and then head across the intervening moorland to Bishop's Seat, clearly seen to the south-west of Eilligan. After enjoying the wild moorland situation, leave the summit and head due south, towards Kilbride Hill, about a mile and a half away. The going is slow, across the rough, mostly pathless ground, though animal tracks will aid progress. Once the Bealach Gaothach is reached, below Kilbride Hill, look for a gap in the forest boundary below. Follow a path on the left hand side of a burn to reach a forest track. It traverses level ground and bears round to the right. A stony path meets it on the left. Follow this down to a more substantial forest track and turn left. In a few hundred yards, keep an eye out for a kissing gate on the right. Go through this and end the walk with a pleasant stroll along either side of the reservoir to return to Dunoon.

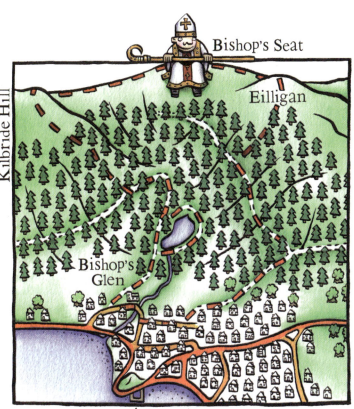

Bishop's Seat

Eilligan

Kilbride Hill

Bishop's Glen

Dunoon

MAP	OS Sheet 63, Firth of Clyde
DISTANCE	6.5 miles (10.5 km)
RATING	Moderate. Tracks and pathless moorland
GEAR	Full hill-walking kit and gaiters

GLENASHDALE FALLS

Given Scotland's propensity for rain, waterfalls often look particularly impressive after a downpour.

THEMES The volume of water cascading over falls can turn them into raging torrents of foam. If they're fairly easy to get to as well, even better – and that's the case with this well-frequented walk on the lovely island of Arran. But Glenashdale Falls, tumbling in a curtain for around 140ft, are not the only attraction on this walk, which is packed with interest. The other major feature apart from the falls is a group of Neolithic tombs called the Giants' Graves – a good example of the chambered burial sites that can be found in many parts of Scotland. About 5,000 years old, these three graves sit in a clearing. They were once roofed but are now open to the elements, and the largest of them comes complete with graffiti from 1883. It's a bit of a trek up a long line of steps to reach them, but worth the effort when you arrive and let your imagination carry you back in time. There's more history, too, in the remains of Whiting Bay Church and an Iron Age hill fort.

ROUTE Park opposite the youth hostel at Whiting Bay, on the shore side of the road. Turn right, then in a short distance left, along the footpath signed to the Giants' Graves and Glenashdale Falls. Continue alongside the burn and through a gate to a signpost directing you left to the Giants' Graves.

Climb the steps – count and see how many you get – to visit the graves and return to the burnside path. Just before the path on the right are the remains of Whiting Bay Church, now largely concealed under vegetation, though some gravestones are still visible. Back on the main path turn left and ascend through woodland alongside the burn, noting the labelled trees of special interest. There are occasional waymarkers for reassurance as you carry on, crossing several bridges. The path begins to rise more steeply to some steps, then a fork. Go right to arrive at the falls and carry on uphill and over a bridge at the top. A conveniently placed picnic table here is handy for a break. Continue into an area of dense pines and through a gap in a wall. You'll reach a sign pointing to the Iron Age fort. Have a look at the ruined ramparts and return to the main path. Cross a bridge next to another waterfall and carry on to a clearing with an open view of the surroundings. Follow the route uphill to a T-junction with a forest road. Turn right and walk on to reach a tarmac road that leads back downhill to Whiting Bay.

Glenashdale Falls

Giant's Graves

Arran

Whiting Bay

MAP	OS Sheet 69, Arran
DISTANCE	3.5 miles (6km)
RATING	Easy. Forest paths and tracks
GEAR	Boots and a waterproof

ST CYRUS TO INVERBERVIE

We have our fair share of brutal crimes committed these days, but looking back through the pages of history can reveal some abhorrent incidents.

THEMES Only ruins now remain of the Kaim of Mathers in St Cyrus, a 15th century castle built by courtier David Barclay, who is linked to a rather gruesome incident. Barclay and other lairds, who detested the local sheriff, lured him to a gully where he was thrown into a cauldron of boiling water. His killers then supped the broth and the gully to this day is still called Sheriff's Kettle. At the other end of the walk, Inverbervie has the status of a royal burgh. The title was bestowed on it in 1341 by King David II and Queen Johanna, who were returning to Scotland from exile in France. Bad weather forced their vessel to land near Inverbervie and they were treated well by the locals, as became their royal status. As a reward, the king gave the town his royal seal of approval. Inverbervie is also the birthplace of Hercules Linton, designer of the famous sailing ship Cutty Sark, now a tourist attraction berthed at Greenwich.

ROUTE From the church in St Cyrus, head along the track to the coast. Turn left and follow the path along the cliff top to a coastal path sign beyond a house. Take care because the path clings to the edge of the cliff and there is a steep drop. The path descends to cross a stone bridge over a burn and goes up to a field. Skirt round the field, passing above a ruined castle, to join a track. Turn left, then right at a junction and descend to the hamlet of Tangelha'. Continue past a caravan park and cross a bridge over a burn. Carry on towards a wartime concrete lookout post. Our route goes through attractively named Seagreens and on to Johnshaven. Make your way along the road between cottages to regain the coast. Stick with the shore road and pass another caravan park to reach a wooden gate. Go through this and walk on, past the grounds of Lathallan School, then a pig farm. A bridge crosses the burn at Haughs Bay and the path arrives at the cottages of Haughs of Benholm. A grassy track continues to Gourdin, another village with a harbour. From here the route winds through a narrow street of cottages and sheds, with the final stretch of open coastline at Horse Crook Bay. Follow the trail to Bervie Bay and Inverbervie. Take the bus back to St Cyrus.

St Cyrus

Johnshaven

Gourdon

Inverbervie

MAP	OS Sheet 45, Stonehaven
DISTANCE	9 miles (15km)
RATING	Moderate. Coastal path
GEAR	Boots and a waterproof

THE WILDCAT TRAIL

Connections with the TV series *Monarch of the Glen* have helped put the Highland community of Newtonmore on the map, and the town has been doing a fine job of promoting itself as a centre for walking.

THEMES The Cairngorms massif proves ample opportunity for those seeking strenuous days in the mountains, getting up to heights of over 4,000ft. The signposted Wildcat Trail offers rather gentler fare. Created as a millennium project using National Lottery funding, it is an excellent low level walk, which can be done in its entirety or split into sections. A well-produced brochure obtainable in the town provides full details. The trail passes through a wonderful variety of scenery, giving views of the Cairngorms and the Monadhliath hills. A stretch alongside the River Spey crosses meadows full of wild flowers in season, including rare orchids. Situated in Badenoch, Newtonmore is proud of its record as one of Scotland's shinty capitals. The team has won the coveted Cammanachd Cup more times than any other. To the west of Newtonmore is the craggy hill of Creag Dubh – the Black Crag. Creag Dubh is the battle cry of the Clan MacPherson, and at the western end of the hill is Cluny's Cave, where the clan chief is reputed to have hidden in safety for nine years after Culloden despite a huge reward of 11,000 Scots pounds for his capture.

ROUTE The trail begins on the western outskirts of Newtonmore, on the A86 approach to the town, where a bridge crosses the River Calder. Follow the path north along the Calder, passing Banchor Cemetery, and into new plantings of native trees.

Continue along a flat, grassy area. Forsaking the river, the trail turns east, then south through Milton Wood, an established conifer plantation. Turn up the access road to Upper Knock and follow the signs, through a section of older birch tree cover. There are superb views over the moorland to the Monadhliath range. Another section of younger birch is reached. Carry on along the path, past the crofting hamlet of Strone and into an attractive gorge. Go through some woodland to the roadside and take the path parallel to it back towards Newtonmore. Just after the Highland Folk Park on the opposite side of the road is a prominent white house. Cross the road and walk south past the house. Ignore the signed Folk Park walk and head left to cross a bridge over the railway line and on to the River Spey, passing around the golf course. Follow the path along the line of the river to complete your circuit back at the Calder Bridge.

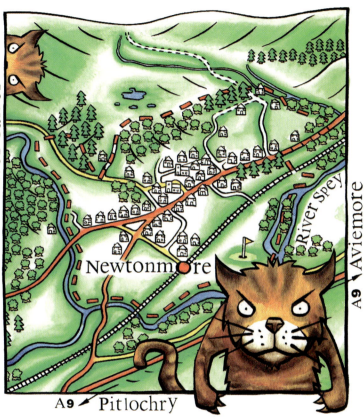

MAP	OS Sheet 35, Kingussie
DISTANCE	7.5 miles (12km)
RATING	Moderate. Paths and tracks
GEAR	Boots and a waterproof

SLIOCH

The photograph almost takes itself. As you drive the road between Gairloch and Kinlochewe, the elements of loch, woodland and mountain combine perfectly in the view across Loch Maree to Slioch.

THEMES The scene must have been captured millions of times. But whereas tourists to the Highlands may well be content with this distant view, hill-walkers champ at the bit to get closer and make a more intimate acquaintance with the mountain whose Gaelic name translates as 'spear'. I'm not sure how it could have acquired such a handle, because there's nothing very spear-like about it. Viewed across Loch Maree it conjures memories of the blancmanges served out of a mould that I got at birthday parties as a child.

But that is not to diminish the stature of this wonderful mountain or the difficulty of getting up close and personal with it. To experience the stupendous view from the top demands a long day's walk that is not for the faint-hearted. The lengthy approach to the lochside has to be repeated on the way out, and by then it feels like a bit of a route march. Nevertheless it's worth it. The view north from Slioch takes in a vast tract of uninhabited wild country. Although seamed by good stalking tracks it is not easily negotiated, thanks to some potentially tricky river crossings. The prize for those hardy souls prepared to venture in to the area is a clutch of six Munros and an acute sense of being at one with the natural environment. The super-fit can attempt a round of all six hills in a day, but to get a real feel for the wilderness I'd recommend a stay of around three days, perhaps using Shenavall bothy as a base.

ROUTE From Incheril, near Kinlochewe village, head north-west along the road, which turns into a track, in the direction of Loch Maree. The route can be boggy in places as it follows the banks of Kinlochewe River. The loch shore is reached and followed briefly before a footbridge crosses the Abhainn an Fhasaigh. Turn right, up Gleann Bianasdail. In about half a mile, near some waterfalls, branch off left to follow a well-worn path upwards, making for the col between Sgurr Dubh and Meall Each. The circuit of ridges around Coire Tuill Bhain, taking in Slioch's summit, is best tackled clockwise to facilitate route finding. Head left on to Slioch's south-east ridge and continue upwards, passing between two lochans, to reach the trig point. Continue clockwise, around to Sgurr an Tuill Bhain, then down to skirt Meall Each to the left. Follow the path back down beside the Abhainn an Fhasaigh to Loch Maree and the long walk out to Incheril.

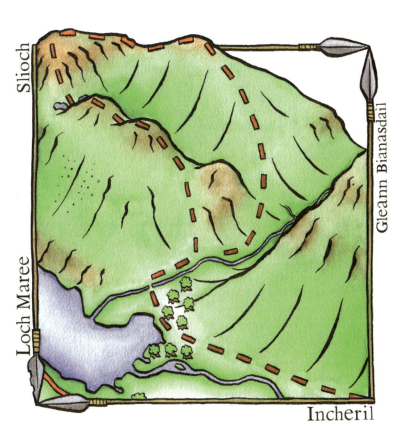

Slioch

Loch Maree

Gleann Bianasdail

Incheril

MAP	OS Sheet 19, Gairloch & Ullapool
DISTANCE	12 miles (19.5km)
RATING	Strenuous. Mostly mountain paths
GEAR	Full hill-walking kit

NORTH THIRD RESERVOIR, BANNOCKBURN

They sent him homeward to think again. King Edward's army was repelled at the battle of Bannockburn in one of the most famous encounters ever on Scottish soil.

THEMES The burn is innocuous enough as burns go. Only when its name is revealed does its true significance become evident, for this is the Bannock Burn, a focal point for the historic battle. King Edward II and his army were defeated by a vastly inferior force in numerical terms, led by Robert the Bruce, who secured his place in history as a national hero, though he nearly lost his life before the battle had even begun. A young English knight, Henry de Bohun, spotted the solitary Bruce patrolling the Scots lines and made a charge, lance lowered, only to be despatched by Bruce's trusty battle axe. In the confrontation between the opposing forces on 24 June, 1314, Bruce's patriotic freedom fighters were facing a formidable English army. But the strategy employed by Bruce, using the landscape to his advantage, was crucial. The English were driven back into the burn and killed or captured. Edward escaped and fled to the security of Dunbar Castle.

ROUTE Finding the start of the walk involves negotiating a complex of minor roads. From the big roundabout near Bannockburn, take the Denny road. Around a mile after the roundabout a turning on the right is signed to Auchenbowie caravan park. Take this road to a junction just past the caravan park and turn left. Follow the road around, ignoring a 'no-through' junction on the left, to arrive at another junction. Turn left towards Carron Bridge. In about a mile the road forks. Take the right-hand fork for the North Third Trout Fishery and continue for about a mile to the brow of a hill with a forestry road on the right. There's a layby for a few cars. Follow the well-defined path to the left of the forestry road. It leads pleasantly uphill through woodland, and in less than half an hour you're on the craggy escarpment above the reservoir. Walk to the trig pillar on Lewis Hill. Continue along the escarpment and drop down into a gorge. Turn left, as indicated by a marker post, to reach the reservoir dam. A path goes right, round the dam base, but many people walk along behind the dam wall. Walk through a field to a gate in the corner, to the road. Follow the road, which at least is quiet, back to the start.

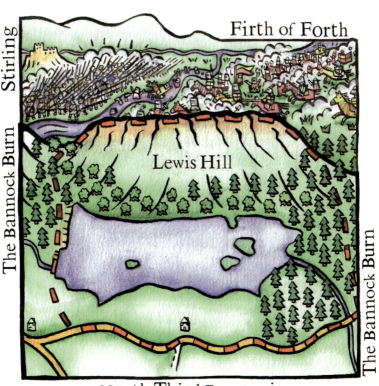

Firth of Forth

Stirling

The Bannock Burn

Lewis Hill

The Bannock Burn

North Third Reservoir

MAP	OS Sheet 5, Stirling and Trossachs
DISTANCE	2.5 miles (4km)
RATING	Easy. Hill path and short road section
GEAR	Boots and a waterproof

SKYE VIEW

Stretches of water pose crossing difficulties for mere mortals. For mythical giants, however, with spears for aid, getting from one side to the other was not such a problem.

THEMES It sounds like a descendant of the dinosaurs you might see in the museum. In fact, as aficionados of the English language will know, a palindrome is a word whose letters spell the same forwards as backwards. A hamlet on the west coast of Scotland bears this distinction. Glenelg sits on the mainland opposite Skye, where the Sound of Sleat meets Kyle Rhea. Both Kyle Rhea and nearby Kyle Akin are supposedly named after legendary giants, who leapt across the narrows using their spears plunged into the water to swing over. Ferries, and now a new bridge, have allowed mere mortals to achieve the same purpose. This walk is a pleasant mix of shoreline and moorland scenery on a circuit that also deviates for a short but sharp climb up Glas Bheinn, with great views across to Skye. South of Glenelg, where the road bends round into Gleann Beag, are Dun Telve and Dun Troddan – the two finest brochs on the mainland. Now only about half their original height, they probably afforded shelter for the locals from marauding Viking invaders. Scotland's biggest broch is Musa Broch in Shetland.

ROUTE From the car park at the Kyle Rhea ferry jetty, take the track north, signed to Ardintoul and Totaig. It passes through gates, staying with the waterline, into a forestry plantation. Where the track forks, go left and pass under a pylon carrying power lines across the water. The track climbs through birch trees and crosses a small gorge, before dropping down to the shoreline again. The broad expanse of Loch Alsh lies ahead as our route takes us alongside the shingle beach, passing fish farm cages offshore. Before Ardintoul Point cut east, inland, to skirt Ardintoul Farm and on to Ardintoul Bay. The track follows the shoreline for a short distance before turning south, away from the bay, to ascend the hillside, with the Allt na Dallach burn down to the left. Continue through woods, climbing to the Bealach Luachrach, the highest point. The peak of Glas Bheinn lies above. To reach it, go through a ride in the forest and out on to the open hillside. Follow an old fence initially. Where this bears off right, strike upwards for Glas Bheinn's summit, with its trig pillar. There are fine views across to Skye, with the peaks of Sgurr na Coinich and Beinn na Caillich prominent in the foreground. Descend again through the forest ride and turn right, following the track downhill through Glen Bernera to reach the coast road leading back to the start.

Loch Alsh Ardintoul Point

Glas Bheinn

Kyle Rhea

Skye

Glenelg

MAP	OS Sheet 33, Loch Alsh & Glen Shiel
DISTANCE	8 miles (13km)
RATING	Moderate. Coast and moorland paths
GEAR	Boots and a waterproof

JAMES HOGG MONUMENT

Literary prowess and the outdoor life, especially agriculture, have been synonymous for Scottish writers and poets, national bard Robert Burns prominent amongst them.

THEMES The affinity between Burns, his environment, the landscape and its creatures stands out clearly in his poetry and songs. Then there's Duncan Ban Macintyre, who wrote about Beinn Dorain above Bridge of Orchy. The remarkable thing about him is that technically speaking he was illiterate, having received no schooling. In the 18th century, education was rudimentary, to say the least, for those living in rural areas and poor communities, and in the case of Macintyre non-existent in a formal sense. For the Ettrick Shepherd, James Hogg, it was much the same. The son of a poor farmer, he hardly received any education, yet his literary achievements are renowned. By his mid-teens he was working as a shepherd, and through ambition and determination had taught himself to read and write.

He started composing poetry while out with the sheep on the hills, drawing on the tradition of local ballads, and came to the attention of Sir Walter Scott, who was travelling the Borders. Although raised in an entirely different social class, Scott became Hogg's mentor. Eventually Hogg moved to Edinburgh and in a few years became recognised as one of the leading poets of

the day. The pull of the Borders was hard to resist, however, and he returned to write the work for which he is best remembered, *The Private Memoirs and Confessions of a Justified Sinner*, published in 1824. His talents brought him the offer of a knighthood but his wife made him turn it down. He died in 1835 and is buried in Ettrick churchyard.

ROUTE From the village hall in Ettrick, turn left along the road to pass the monument to Hogg. Continue to the war memorial. Turn right past the church and walk uphill with Kirk Burn on your right and Craig Hill on your left. Maintain your direction, heading for low ground ahead. Carry on to reach the Slunk, a heavily eroded burn, from where there are superb views up the Ettrick Valley. Cross the Slunk using stones to help keep your feet dry. At a wire fence bear left to reach a metal fingerpost marked Riskinhope. Cross a stile and descend along the other side of the fence to reach the Southern Upland Way long distance path. From here it's a straightforward matter of following the Way, between Scabcleuch Burn on your left and Scabcleuch Hill on the right, to reach the road. Turn left back to the start.

Scabcleuch Hill

Craig Hill

Kirk Burn

Ettrick

MAP	OS Sheet 79, Hawick and Eskdales
DISTANCE	4.5 miles (7km)
RATING	Easy. Hill tracks and moorland
GEAR	Full hill-walking kit

CREAG MEAGAIDH

The repair of popular mountain paths has been going on for many years, and has helped to redress the problem of erosion on vulnerable ground.

THEMES I can claim to have made a practical difference to underfoot conditions for walkers heading up to the great cliffs of Coire Ardair, under Creag Meagaidh. At the time I was a member of Oban Mountaineering Club, and we spent a day improving the boggy lower reaches of the footpath, digging drains and mending the surface. My working partner Chris Warwick and I became pretty adept at building cross-drains as a result, having previously gained experience on a similar project in Glencoe. Footpath 'improvements' in mountain areas are a controversial subject, and some purists might argue that paths should be left completely alone. Most walkers agree, however, that as long as things are sensitively done there's nothing wrong with making underfoot conditions more pleasant and appealing to the eye.
Old railway sleepers have been laid along substantial stretches of the path to Coire Ardair. Perhaps this is not the most sightly solution to the problem, but it has succeeded in allowing the vegetation on either side to regenerate. It's part of an ongoing programme of estate management set in motion after the land was bought over for the nation in 1985. It also means that access is unrestricted all year round, even during the stalking season.

ROUTE From the big car park on the north-west side of Loch Laggan, head along the path towards the corrie, skirting Aberarder Farm. It's a long but pleasant approach, passing between the hills on either side, ending with a view of the towering cliffs – the domain of winter climbers who test their skills on the snow-filled gullies and icy crags. If time is short or the weather foul, you can end your walk here and return by the same route. For Creag Meagaidh's summit, head for the notch in the skyline on the right, known as The Window, to reach a bealach. Then turn left – south – and climb the ridge ahead to a plateau. Direction-finding here can be tricky in poor visibility, so make sure your map and compass skills are up to date. Follow the broad ridge south-west to the top. Now there's a choice to be made – whether to return by the same line or take the ridge to the right of Coire Ardair, which ends with an easy descent off Sron a' Ghoire towards the farm. A bridge crosses the Allt Coire Ardair just west of the farm buildings. Whichever option is chosen, take great care to steer clear of the cliffs when skirting the corrie. Both walkers and climbers have disappeared over the edge in the past, with very nasty consequences.

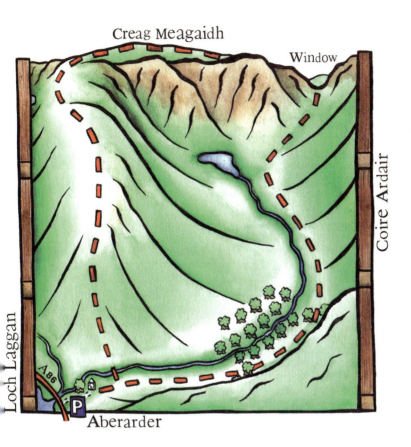

Creag Meagaidh

Window

Coire Ardair

Loch Laggan

A 86

Aberarder

MAP	OS Sheet 34, Fort Augustus
DISTANCE	9.5 miles (15km)
RATING	Strenuous. Hill paths
GEAR	Full hill-walking kit

CUL MOR

The Inchnadamph area of Assynt has caves that have yielded fascinating finds on the history of human habitation.

THEMES Driving north from Ullapool is almost like entering another world – an elemental landscape comprising mountains and water. This is prime territory for walkers. If you're looking for a good introduction to the area, Cul Mor is as good a choice as any hill. With the distinction of being the highest Corbett in Assynt, it's contained within the Inverpolly National Nature Reserve and is easily accessible from the road via an improved stalkers' path. The geology of Scotland is such that it does not have extensive cave systems. However, the Inchnadamph area of Assynt is an exception. The so-called Bone Caves here were first excavated in 1889 by two geologists – Peach and Horne. They found human remains dating back 10,000 years. The bones of reindeer, arctic fox, lynx, brown bear and numerous rodents have also been discovered – some dating back much further than the human specimens. The caves are located south of Inchnadamph and due east of Canisp at grid reference NC 268170. Reaching them involves a walk of about a mile from the A837, but it is unwise to venture into the caverns without the proper knowledge and equipment.

ROUTE From the visitor centre on the A835 north of Ullapool, walk north along the road for a short distance to pick up a refurbished stalkers' path on the left. It rises gradually, passing Lochan Fhionnlaidh. Continue to where the path fades into the broad ridge of Meallan Diomhainn. Carry on upwards, curving round to the right to reach a small lochan – a good navigational aid in mist. From here a ridge climbs steeply south along the edge of craggy Coire Gorm. Pass a little awkwardly through a boulder field to reach the summit of Cul Mor, marked by a trig pillar inside a wall that offers shelter from the wind. The unmistakable form of Suilven lies due north and the equally distinctive cone of Stac Pollaidh to the west. From Cul Mor's top, stick with the line of Coire Gorm and head down, turning south to a bealach under Creag nan Calman, Cul Mor's twin summit, though lower than the main top. Now curve carefully round to the east, dropping down into the shallow corrie below, using Meallan Diomhainn as a directional guide. Cross the burn issuing from the corrie to regain the top of Meallan Diomhainn and retrace your outward route back.

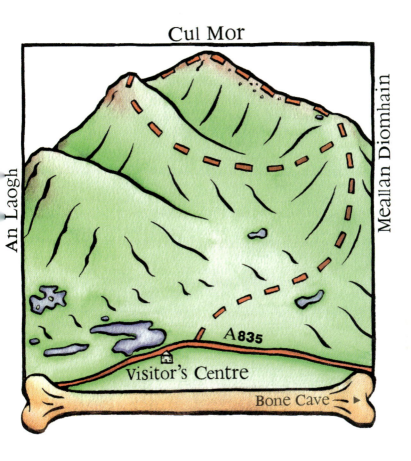

Cul Mor

An Laogh

Meallan Diomhain

A835

Visitor's Centre

Bone Cave →

MAP	OS Sheet 15, Loch Assynt
DISTANCE	6.5 miles (11km)
RATING	Strenuous. Mountain paths
GEAR	Full hill-walking kit

PENTLANDS LOCHS

The Ministry of Defence is not used to losing battles, but a proposed extension to its training area in the Pentlands raised a public outcry so fierce that it was forced to concede defeat.

THEMES It was a well organised campaign, fronted by the Ramblers' Association's Scottish branch, that caused the Ministry to back down. The strength of feeling generated was an indication of how well-loved the Pentlands are for the people of Edinburgh and its surrounds. Like Holyrood Park in the centre of the city and Arthur's Seat, the hills offer urban dwellers a valuable and much needed green lung, with opportunities for miles of walking. Kings, saints and gentry all have connections with the Pentlands. Beneath the waters of Glencorse Reservoir – one of four passed on this walk that act as a water supply for the capital's populace – lie the remains of the Chapel of St Catherine's in the Hopes, dating back to the 13th century and the reign of Robert the Bruce. It has a parallel in other parts of Britain, notably Wales and the Lake District, where whole villages were flooded for the sake of water provision and in exceptionally dry spells come to the surface again – reviving ghosts of the past. At the start of the walk, alongside Edinburgh's busy city bypass, is Bonaly Tower. It was the last home of Lord Cockburn, who made these hills a favourite haunt and wrote: "Unless some avenging angel shall expel me, I shall never leave that paradise."

ROUTE From the car park at the end of Bonaly Road, follow signs in the direction of Easter Kinleith, making for the first of our four reservoirs – Torduff. Walk along past the dam and, with the reservoir on your left, continue to its end, then follow the shore of neighbouring Clubbiedean Reservoir.

The path turns right between fields and under a line of pylons to reach Easter Kinleith farm, with the community of Currie beyond. At the farm the path bends left, signposted Harlaw. Continue over a bridge and look out for a large white house called Crossroads.

Turn sharp left, following the sign for Glencorse Reservoir, passing a conifer plantation. The route continues across open ground to a small stand of conifers before the northern tip of Glencorse Reservoir and its dog-leg shape is reached. After visiting the reservoir, backtrack slightly and veer right, taking the sign to Colinton and Bonaly. The going is uphill as the path cuts between Harbour Hill on the left and Capelaw Hill on the right, down to Bonaly Reservoir. Then it's an easy downhill jaunt, with the city spread out ahead, back to the start.

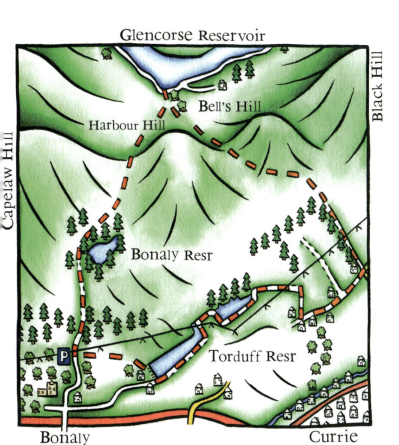

Glencorse Reservoir

Black Hill

Capelaw Hill

Bell's Hill

Harbour Hill

Bonaly Resr

Torduff Resr

P

Bonaly

Currie

MAP	OS Sheet 66, Edinburgh, Penicuik and N. Berwick
DISTANCE	7 miles (11km)
RATING	Moderate. Tracks, can be muddy in places
GEAR	Boots and take a waterproof

MEIKLE BALLOCH HILL

Food and drink, in the form of fish from the sea, wholesome soups and whisky, characterise the coastal area from Aberdeen to Inverness.

THEMES Fishing has always been a staple industry of the north east. The entire coast between Aberdeen and Inverness, along the Moray Firth, is peppered with fishing towns and villages of varying sizes and lots of local character. There are a number of visitor attractions and museums well worth taking a look at if you're in the area, and you want to learn more about how essential fishing has been to these communities. There's plenty of good walking too, both on the coast and inland, and this route takes us up a little hill near Keith. Despite being not much above 1,000ft, it offers wonderful views. Those with a taste for the amber nectar have a veritable reservoir of the stuff on offer in these parts. Strathisla Distillery on the outskirts of Keith is the oldest working distillery in the Highlands, and one of eight on a 70-mile malt whisky trail on the northern side of the Grampians. Staying on the food and drink theme, there's the Baxters soup factory and visitor centre, close to Fochabers. George Baxter, at one-time a gardener at Gordon Castle, started the business in 1868 which has since become a household name.

ROUTE To walk off the excesses of all that food and drink, from Keith town centre take a minor road to Herricks water treatment works. Just past the works turn left and park at the side of a forestry track. Follow the higher of two tracks uphill, and at a track junction turn right. Continue and look out for a pole on the left at the bottom of a narrow path through a firebreak. Take this path through the wood and on up to the summit of Meikle Balloch with its extensive panorama. Once you have drunk your fill of the view and enjoyed a well-deserved bite to eat, follow the path south along the top of the hill and into the plantation again. At a track junction shortly after a clearing, fork right, downhill, to pass a quarry. At the next track junction turn right and almost immediately left. At the forest edge turn right along an old military road, with the plantation on your right and pastureland on the left. A gate is reached. Go through it, then turn right for Mains of Birkenburn farm and on to Bridge of Tarnash. Just before the bridge, go down concrete steps on the right and through woodland to the Falls of Tarnash. Cross an iron bridge and walk on by the burn to another bridge. Bend left uphill to a junction and turn right. About a quarter of a mile further on, turn right again to follow the road leading back to the start point.

Keith

Tarnash

Meikle Balloch

Whisky & Soup

Meikle Balloch

MAP	OS Sheet 28, Elgin and Dufftown
DISTANCE	7 miles (11km)
RATING	Moderate. Well-used tracks and paths
GEAR	Full hill-walking kit

CRAIGELLACHIE NATURE RESERVE

Nature reserves offer the opportunity to walk and learn more about plants and wildlife at the same time. Here's a little gem hidden away on a hillside at Aviemore.

THEMES Consider the Cairngorms and thoughts of high-level walks on the gusty summits spring to mind. But there is gentler fare to be savoured here too, and Aviemore has its own mini ridge walk above a National Nature Reserve. Easily missed unless you look carefully, Craigellachie NNR is Aviemore's very own secret garden. It offers a treasure trove of natural delights equalling those of the famous children's story by Frances Hodgson Burnett. It's a great place to spend half a day rambling through the lovely birchwoods, spotting wild flowers – including delicate orchids – and doing some bird-watching. Peregrine falcons are regular nesting visitors. The ridge above the reserve is a brilliant vantage point for viewing the Cairngorm massif. The great cleft of the Lairig Ghru is easy to spot, as are the cars of the funicular railway, looking like Dinky toys from this distance. Controversially, walkers are not allowed to use the funicular to gain access to the tops.

ROUTE From the outskirts of the town, follow the road towards the youth hostel and turn right, along a path that gives access to the nature reserve through a corrugated metal tunnel under the A9. Immediately after the tunnel is an information board on the left. Continue into the reserve, past the remains of an oak tree with details about the history of the woodland, which was once populated by oaks. They have since been replaced naturally by birch trees. Follow the green arrow to meander along a path that undulates through the birches and eventually makes a descent to a track. Ignore the green arrow pointing right here and instead turn left, uphill, passing an enclosed water board reservoir.

Stay with the path as it climbs upwards towards the ridge ahead. Keep left where the path divides on some fairly steep ground in a shallow gully. Carry on to the crest of the ridge and traverse along it in a southerly direction. Sizeable cairns mark the line, which includes Craigellachie summit. Those who wish can follow the path round to the end, being careful not to stray too close to the crags passed at the beginning of the walk. From here retrace your steps to the track. At the green arrow ignored earlier, continue straight on to reach another arrow pointing right. Follow the path to pass a loch, then another loch down to the left, and back to the start.

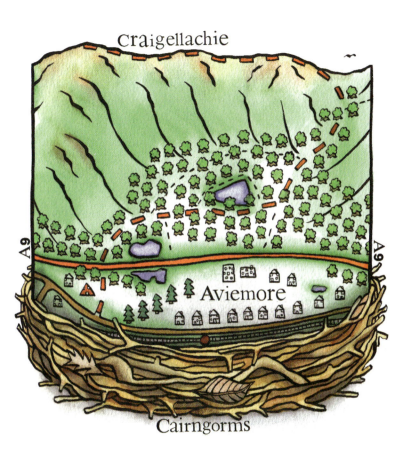

Craigellachie

Aviemore

Cairngorms

MAP	OS Sheet 36, Grantown, Aviemore & Cairngorm
DISTANCE	4 miles (6km)
RATING	Easy. Nature reserve and hill paths
GEAR	Boots and a waterproof

BEINN A' BHEITHIR

The village of Ballachulish suffers from something of a split personality, as it is divided by Loch Leven. Looking down on it is the Hill of the Thunderbolt.

THEMES As a queen who liked to meander about the Highlands, Victoria was impressed by a visit to Ballachulish – its two halves now joined by a bridge rather than the ferry service which once plied across the straits. The queen's diary entry makes note of the lengths to which the villagers went in decorating the place for her visit. It makes note of something else – slate quarrying. From the early 1700s Ballachulish was the site of a major operation which continued for more than 250 years until 1955, when the quarries closed. Then it must have been much more of an industrial setting and a hive of labour-intensive activity. These days it is rather more green and in keeping with the surrounding landscape. Ballachulish is dominated by the dramatically named Hill of the Thunderbolt, Beinn a' Bheithir, whose twin peaks are both Munros. A climb of this shapely mountain also provides an opportunity for a short exploration of the village. As well as tourism, modern economic activity in Ballachulish includes the production of harps by the company Starfish Designs. At South Ballachulish, overlooking the bridge, is a monument to James Stewart, who was hanged at the spot for the murder of Colin Campbell of Glenure – a crime he did not commit.

His story was the basis of Robert Louis Stevenson's novel *Kidnapped*.

ROUTE Beinn a' Bheithir offers walkers a variety of options, and if transport can be arranged I'd recommend a traverse towards the west for stunning sunsets. The most popular ascent is from the small clutch of houses at South Ballachulish, reached off the Oban road just west of Ballachulish Bridge. Follow a forestry track on the right hand side of Gleann a Ghaolais, above the burn. Continue straight on, ignoring any offshoot tracks, climbing up past a disused quarry on the left. At a junction go straight across and continue to a concrete bridge. After the bridge a cairn marks the path leading up to the bealach between Beinn a' Bheithir's twin summits. In its final stages the path is steep and bouldery. From the bealach turn right and climb Sgorr Dhonuill, at 3,284ft. Return to the bealach and climb Sgorr Dhearg ahead, slightly higher at 3,360ft. Leave the summit and descend along the north ridge, back towards South Ballachulish. Follow the ridge all the way down to a clearing above a forest track. Drop down to the track and turn right to emerge, in just over half a mile, on the A82 east of Ballachulish Bridge. Turn left to regain the start point.

MAP	OS Sheet 41, Ben Nevis
DISTANCE	9 miles (14km)
TERRAIN	Strenuous. Rough mountain paths
GEAR	Full hill-walking kit

BEINN EDRA

From the Skye hamlet of Uig, the hopping-off point for ferries sailing to the Western Isles, climb up to the Trotternish Ridge for dramatic views.

THEMES Drive the road that winds round Skye's northern extremity, the Trotternish Peninsula, and there is endless fascination. There's the pinnacle of the Old Man of Storr, the strange formations of the Quiraing, Kilt Rock, with its sheer buttresses resembling the folds of a kilt, Flora Macdonald's monument and much more. Down the middle of the peninsula runs the Trotternish Ridge – a long switchback like a crooked spine. About 20 miles long, it provides a challenging outing for anyone bold and fit enough to tackle it all in a day. The views are awe-inspiring. Our walk samples just a short section of the ridge and takes in its highest point – Beinn Edra – reached from the hamlet of Uig, tucked in a bay on the west coast of Trotternish. It's the busy ferry port for the Western Isles, linking Skye with Lochmaddy on North Uist and Tarbert on Harris, and also serves to accommodate local fishing vessels. A road was constructed to Uig from Portree in 1812, and by 1840 a pier had been built, with steamers providing regular services to Tarbert and other north-west Scotland destinations. The steamers were replaced by a car ferry in 1961. The Skye Brewery is sited at Uig, making its own real ales including Red Cuillin, named after the range of hills in the south.

Captain Fraser's Folly sits above the bay. It dates from the 1890s, and was built by the laird of the day.

ROUTE From Uig, walk along the minor road up Glen Conon, which joins the A865 at a road bridge over the River Conon. The gradient is steep to begin with as the road goes through sharp bends. It undulates past cottages before coming to an end. A track strikes ahead over a stile and continues across open moorland. Waterfalls cascade through a rocky amphitheatre down to your right. Some marshy ground comes next, crossed by a rather ill-defined path. A fence is reached, running at right angles. Cross it and walk down to the Lon Airigh-uige burn. Follow a path east, alongside the burn, with the Trotternish Ridge straight ahead. Make for it, climbing up to Bealach Uige. Once on the crest of the ridge, turn right on to the summit of Beinn Edra, keeping well away from the steep drop on your left. A trig pillar, inside a stone circle, marks the top. Descend south and stay on the path, bearing right, back towards Uig. Continue along the line of the Lon an t-Stratha burn to a croft at Balnaknock. Follow a track, which soon becomes a minor road, down to the A856. Turn right back to regain the start.

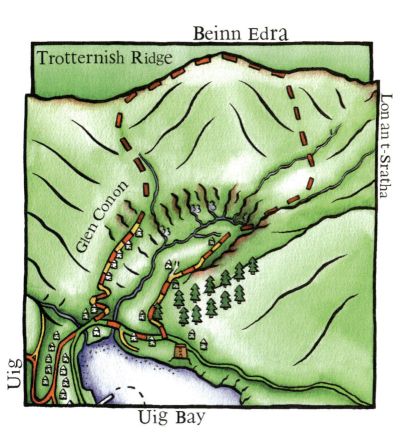

Beinn Edra

Trotternish Ridge

Lon an t-Sratha

Glen Conon

Uig

Uig Bay

MAP	OS Sheet 23, North Skye
DISTANCE	7.5 miles (12km)
RATING	Moderate. Minor road, tracks and paths
GEAR	Full hill-walking kit

CORWHARN

You may not actually be flying, like Peter Pan, but getting up high on the rolling Angus hills can provide some wonderful vistas.

THEMES He was the man who never wanted to grow up, who wrote about the boy who never did grow up. James Matthew Barrie was born in 1860 in the Angus burgh of Kirriemuir, and is best remembered for his children's fantasy *Peter Pan*, written as a play and adapted for cinema and television. It's a timeless tale enjoyed by millions of youngsters everywhere as they are transported to Neverland. Barrie wrote a string of successful novels and plays, and Kirriemuir featured in early stories under the fictional name of Thrums. But Peter flies high above everything else, and still provides financial benefit to the renowned Great Ormond Street children's hospital in London. The author donated the rights of the stage production to the hospital. Barrie died in 1937 and is buried in Kirriemuir next to his parents, sister and brother David, who died after a skating accident when James was a small boy. Our walk takes in the Angus hills, not far from Kirriemuir, starting alongside Backwater Reservoir, which has supplied water to Angus residents for more than 30 years. It was opened by the Queen in 1969, and holds 25 million cubic metres of water behind the dam, which extends to 800 metres. A circuit of the

reservoir is a pleasant walk in itself, but like Peter Pan, our route rises higher.

ROUTE From the car park on the north-eastern side of the reservoir, walk south for a short distance along the road to the end of a plantation and turn left, through a gate. Continue to another gate, with the ruined farm of Ley below. Cut across a field to a fence, with two gates set in it. Go through the left-hand one to gain a grassy track. Turn left along the track and on to a rocky path through a narrow gorge. Continue through a gate and a field to the road in Glen Quharity. Turn left along the road to Longdrum, continuing via a track. Where it branches, take the left fork, and climb up beside some woodland. Follow the ridge towards the highest point on Milldewan Hill and contour round the top to a fence. Follow this to the summit of Cairn Corse, then to the neat cairn on Corwharn. Cross the stile on the summit where two fences meet. A ridge curves round to the left down to a bealach. Continue west to meet a track that crosses the Hole Burn and rises to the edge of Drumshade plantation. Carry on along the track, which eventually exits the trees and continues west past Glenhead Lodge to Hole, then Glenhead Farm. Keep left to return to the start.

MAP	OS Sheet 44, Ballater
DISTANCE	10 miles (12.5 km)
RATING	Moderate. Hill paths, track and road
GEAR	Full hill-walking kit

19

THE HERMITAGE & RUMBLING BRIDGE

Ossian's Hall, near Dunkeld, is an intriguing place. Built in 1758 by the nephew of the second Duke of Atholl, it's a small folly above the River Braan, with a stunning view of waterfalls.

THEMES It's not especially difficult to imagine, in the mid 1780s, visitors entering the hall to be greeted by a painting of Ossian, the Celtic bard, serenading a group of maidens. Then came gasps of awe as the guide operated a device that withdrew the painting into the wall, providing access to another room – a hall of mirrors – giving the illusion of water pouring all around, reflecting the river cascading outside. The structure was damaged in 1869 but was later presented to the National Trust for Scotland in 1944 by Katherine, Duchess of Atholl and thankfully restored, though these days minus its painting and the mirrors. A little further on from the hall is Ossian's Cave, a great place for children to wriggle into, that adds further excitement to the day.

ROUTE Take the A822 Crieff road off the A9 near Dunkeld and turn immediately right, signed Inver. Take a left fork to cross the railway and stop at a car park on the right just after this. Follow the path signposted to the Hermitage and wander through woodland to a bridge crossing the Braan, with Ossian's Hall on the other side. Continue along the bank of the river to the cave. After this the path veers right, away from the river. Cross over a main track and after a short distance curve left. Go on again, then turn left on to a clear track. Follow this to cross a little bridge over the Craigvinean burn, heading for Rumbling Bridge on a wide, grassy path. This meets a lane. Turn left downhill for Rumbling Bridge, where the Braan is regained. Walk along the road a short way and turn left on a narrow path into woodland. Follow it, high above the river, until it turns right to meet the A822. Cross this and continue on the track ahead until just before a cattle grid. Go through a gate on the left on to another track and continue past Tomgarrow settlement to enter Tomgarrow Wood. Go round Tomgarrow Cottage and on to a gate in a deer fence into conifer forest. Shortly, turn left along a main track and go straight over a path junction on a broad track. At a major track junction make a U-turn left and at the next junction go right on the main track. Continue to the A822. Cross it and follow the track ahead down to a minor road and the car park at the start.

Rumbling Bridge

Tomgarrow

A 822

Ossian's
Hall

P

A 9

Dunkeld

MAP	OS Sheet 52, Pitlochry and Aberfeldy
DISTANCE	5 miles (8 km)
RATING	Easy. Mostly forest tracks and paths
GEAR	Boots recommended

20

BEN LAWERS

This mountain group holds an abundance of prizes for seekers after Munros, and while many walkers confine themselves to Beinn Ghlas and Ben Lawers, there are prospects for longer outings too.

THEMES Ben Lawers is only 16ft short of 4,000ft, and that must have been too much of a temptation for Glasgow resident Malcolm Ferguson who tried, back in 1878, to make up the deficit. One summer's day he marshalled 30 men and two masons to build a 20ft cairn on the summit. A fairly substantial remnant of it is left, together with an indicator disc. While there's no doubting that Ben Lawers is a wonderful hill to climb, it is a victim of its own popularity, and the well-beaten path to the top has suffered erosion problems over the years. Some blame is laid at the door of the National Trust for Scotland's visitor centre sited beneath the mountain on the narrow road that links Loch Tay and Glen Lyon. The centre has become known as the Starship Enterprise by those who believe it is out of place in its surroundings. Supporters claim it helps to educate people, fostering a greater understanding of mountains and conservation, and it provides information on the mountain environment, flora and fauna. If you want to avoid the crowds, steer clear of the peak summer season for a more enjoyable walk, although early summer brings the benefit of seeing beautiful alpine flowers.

ROUTE From the car park at the visitor centre, follow the wooden walkway until it divides. One branch takes the gentle nature trail and the other is signposted for Ben Lawers. The path keeps to the right of the delightfully named Burn of Edramucky, issuing from Coire Odhar above. Continue to where zig-zags allow the path to be tackled more easily up the slopes of Beinn Ghlas's west ridge. It's a stiff pull until the way flattens before a final burst of energy must be mustered to reach the top of Beinn Ghlas – around 300ft lower than Ben Lawers. The satisfaction of gaining a Munro summit is tempered somewhat by the fact that height now has to be sacrificed to reach our final goal. Descend from Beinn Ghlas to the col joining the two peaks and gird your loins for the assault on Lawers. As you climb, work on the path to help combat erosion becomes evident. Finally there is reward for all the hard work with one of the finest views from a Munro anywhere in Scotland. Sitting serenely in the corrie to the north-west is the Lochan nan Cat, and further below, stretching in a long line between Killin to the west and Kenmore to the east is Loch Tay, while mountains range all around. Return by the same route.

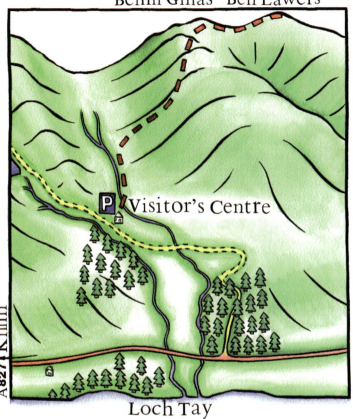

Beinn Ghlas   Ben Lawers

Visitor's Centre

Killin

A827

Loch Tay

MAP	OS Sheet 51, Loch Tay
DISTANCE	5 miles (8km)
RATING	Strenuous. Mountain paths
GEAR	Full hill-walking kit

21

BROUGHTON HEIGHTS

Transport yourself into the world of thriller writer John Buchan as you wander over the hills that inspired his tales of intrigue.

THEMES He was a writer who enjoyed the hills and invented one of the most famous characters in wartime thriller history – Richard Hannay, the expatriate Scot with an English stiff upper lip and an uncanny ability to extricate himself from sticky situations. Hannay starred in John Buchan's best-known work, the *Thirty-Nine Steps*, subsequently the basis for three films. Alfred Hitchcock directed the first in 1935, starring Robert Donat as Hannay, widely acknowledged as the best. Kenneth Moore adopted the role in the 1959 version and Robert Powell starred in the most recent in 1978. A son of the manse, John Buchan was born in Perth in 1875, but his grandparents lived in the Borders village of Broughton, near Biggar, where the author spent summer holidays. Undoubtedly the lovely hill country around the village inspired his tales of derring-do, which he liked to call "shockers". Richard Hannay was based on the real-life military spy William Ironside. These days, Buchan is not only remembered through a visitor centre in Broughton but also in a 13-mile walk, signposted between the village and Peebles.

ROUTE Approaching Broughton village on the A701 from Edinburgh, look for a sign saying 'Art Gallery and Tea Room'.

Turn left and follow the single track road uphill to a walkers' car park next to a cottage. Walk north along the grassy track, passing Duck Pond Plantation on the left. Continue on, fording a small burn, to reach a path junction. Bear left, uphill towards a dip on the skyline between Clover Law and Broomy Side. A signpost is reached marking the John Buchan Way off to the right. Keep left, walking on up to a gate and stile. Cross the stile and turn right, following the undulating hill path over Broomy Side and Green Law, finally reaching the trig pillar on Broughton Heights. Go straight on, then curve round to the right, descending alongside a forestry plantation. Ascend Brown Dod, then Flint Hill. There's no obvious single path off this, though sheep tracks will help facilitate your descent to a broad, flat area with Stobo Hopehead Farm straight ahead. Walk towards a fence and turn right along it, crossing rushy ground to a gate and track. Turn right along the track to a circular, walled sheep fank. Pick up an indistinct path alongside this that winds over easy ground on the right hand side of the valley. Near the upper end of this, cross over on to the John Buchan Way and turn right along it back to the outward route, which is followed to the start.

MAP	OS Sheet 72, Upper Clyde Valley
DISTANCE	6.5 miles (11km)
RATING	Moderate. Moorland paths and tracks
GEAR	Full hill-walking kit

22

THE BADENOCH WAY

Long distance path walking is not everyone's cup of tea, but although designated as a "way" this one strikes a good compromise and can be done easily in a day.

THEMES Scotland's best known long distance path, the West Highland Way, takes a bit of a pounding under the multitude of feet making the journey from Milngavie to Fort William. It's a good thing that other routes have been created in more recent years to take some of the pressure off and introduce the uninitiated to different scenery. The Badenoch Way, on Speyside, is one of them. Nothing like as strenuous an undertaking as the west Highland mammoth, it has some beautiful stretches of walking with very little ascent and generally firm surfaces underfoot, barring one section through forestry. It's a linear route, so a car at either end is required – or it's possible to catch a bus linking Kingussie and the Dalraddy caravan site at the eastern end of the walk (contact Traveline on 0870-6082 608 or Citylink on 08705 50 50 50 for details). The caravan site, a couple of miles from the village of Kincraig, has a car park, and an information leaflet on the Way describes the walk in this direction.

ROUTE At the caravan site and the first waymarker, cross Dalraddy Moor, keeping an eye out for marker posts, heading generally south-west towards the River Spey and the corner of a plantation. The waymarking is not as clear as it could be, so take care. Follow a path through caledonian pines, with good waymarking. Reaching a railway embankment, turn left through a gate and head on to a delectable section of the route high above the Spey through an open birch wood, with superb views over to the Cairngorms. Go past Kincraig Stores to cross a road bridge over the Spey. Continue to Loch Insh Watersports Centre and through some very pleasant RSPB woodland to cross the B970. Forest Enterprise paths then lead up towards Farleiter Hill and a rather boggy section of path through pine forest. Don't let this spoil your enjoyment though, because things improve again. Emerge from the plantation on to a broad forestry road and turn right, downhill to a track that passes through the hamlets of Inveruglas and Drumguish, offering fine views of the Monadhliath hills to the north. A bridge over the tumbling waters of the River Tromie leads in to the RSPB's Insh Marshes reserve through a gate on the right, and another lovely stretch of walking to finish at a car park near Ruthven Barracks – worth a visit before ending your day, perhaps at a local hostelry or tea shop.

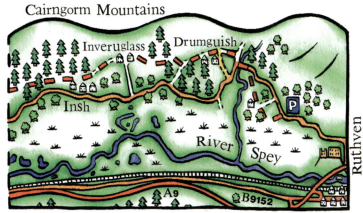

MAP	OS Sheet 35, Kingussie
DISTANCE	10 miles (16km)
RATING	Moderate. Waymarked paths and quiet roads
GEAR	Hill-walking kit advised

23

LAGGAN HILL & LADY MARY'S WALK

Sir Patrick Murray of Ochtertyre must have been very fond of his daughter, Lady Mary, to create such a lovely walk for her on the banks of the River Earn in Perthshire.

THEMES Lined on either side with majestic beeches, the avenue of Lady Mary's Walk is a wonderfully tranquil place to forget your troubles and enjoy the peace of the river flowing by. Established in 1815, it is well used by locals and visitors to Crieff, and combined with Laggan Hill gives a splendid easy circuit. Seats carved with verses – many referring to Lady Mary and her obvious empathy with the scenery – have been placed at strategic intervals along the route. Lady Mary's life was undoubtedly a lot less stressful than that of General Sir David Baird, who fought in India with the 73rd Highlanders in 1779. He was captured but survived to return and fight again 12 years later. A monument commemorating his military exploits sits on a hill top and is worth taking in on the walk. Sir David was a fine, upstanding character if the inscription on the towering obelisk is to be believed.

ROUTE Start the walk from the large car park in Taylor Park, Crieff. Cross the bridge over the River Turret and take the first turning left into Laggan Road. A signpost points the way to Laggan Hill. Pass through houses to another signpost pointing right, by a cottage. Continue along the lane to the top of Laggan Hill. Carry straight on past Puddock Pond on the right – 'puddock' being the Scots word for frog. At a track junction just after this, turn left and continue straight on through the trees to a clearing with a view ahead of the River Earn. The path narrows and continues through quite dense pines and birches, veering round very gradually to the left. The Baird monument is on the hill to the left. Look for a rather indistinct path leading up to it. Return to continue downhill in a southerly direction. Keep an eye out for the roof of a cottage through the trees below, to the right. At a track junction turn right and walk down to the road by the cottage. Turn left, then immediately left again on another track, passing Trowan Farm, heading back towards Crieff. Carry on between fields to a ruined building and a signpost indicating the way on to Lady Mary's Walk. Follow the walk, sticking close to the river where the track divides further on. The River Turret flows in to the Earn from the left by a gate. Go through the gate and take the path alongside the Turret to complete the circuit at the road bridge.

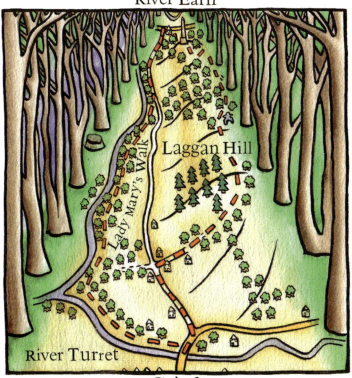

River Earn

Laggan Hill

Lady Mary's Walk

River Turret

Crieff

MAP	OS Sheet 58, Pitlochry to Crieff
DISTANCE	5.5 miles (9km)
RATING	Easy. Woodland and riverside paths
GEAR	Boots and a waterproof

24

ST MONANS TO CRAIL

There's no doubting the charm of Fife's East Neuk. Each village has its hallmarks, and on a sunny day there is no finer walking to be had than a stroll along the seashore.

THEMES There is a lot to see on this stretch of the Fife Coastal Path, which follows the coastline between the Forth and Tay bridges. At 78 miles it offers a great holiday walk spread over a few days. This section, from St Monans to Crail, is one of the most attractive, and public transport is readily available for the return. Almost immediately you set off there's something to distract the attention in St Monans, as you pass the restored windmill that pumped sea water into salt pans. Their remains are still visible. It took 32 tons of sea water to produce 1 ton of salt. The Gyles House at Pittenweem was built in the first half of the 17th century for Captain James Cook, who carried Charles II to France after his defeat at the battle of Worcester. Anstruther, or 'Ainster' in local parlance, had a thriving fishing port until after the Second World War, when the decline in herring fishing led to its demise, though there is some smaller-scale activity today. The Dreel Burn, which separates Wester and Easter Anstruther, is celebrated in folklore. A sturdy beggar woman carried King James V across it to stop him getting his feet wet: her reward – a purse of gold. Crail, with its chocolate box cottages, finishes off the walk.

ROUTE Car parking in St Monans is available close to the start of the walk. A good path heads past the windmill and on to Pittenweem. Follow coastal path signs to the east end of the village and along a field edge, before descending a flight of stone steps back to the coastline. Continue along the edge of the golf course to Anstruther. Facing the Scottish Fisheries Museum opposite the harbour car park, turn right and walk along the street, staying parallel to the sea front. Shore Street ends at a children's playground. Walk on, passing a caravan park and a free-range pig farm, where the hilarious antics of tiny piglets are yet another distraction. The route is easy to follow as you take in the sights and sounds of the coast – the screech of oystercatchers and the haunting cry of curlews. The prominent landmark of Caiplie Coves is a series of eroded sandstone pillars forming caves. The largest contains crosses carved into the walls, thought to date back to early Christian times. Follow the path to the right, further along passing the remains of a saltworks. The path weaves its way between rocks until Crail finally comes into view. There's a bus stop in the main street near a butcher's shop for the return.

MAP	OS Sheet 59, St Andrews
DISTANCE	7 miles (11km)
RATING	Easy. Seashore path
GEAR	Boots recommended. Take a waterproof

THREE BRETHREN

They stand in a cluster, like three old men having an earnest conversation on a street corner. Except these three cairns, around 10ft high and over 1,500ft up, mark the summit of a hill top near Selkirk which bears their name – Three Brethren.

THEMES The carefully constructed cairns, dwarfing the little white Ordnance Survey trig pillar, symbolise the meeting of three old states: Yair and Philliphaugh districts and Selkirk Burgh. Each year the Selkirk Standard Bearer and his entourage ride on horseback to the Brethren as they engage in the Common Riding tradition. If the cairns could talk, they would doubtless tell many tales of the drovers who traversed these hills years ago, moving their cattle to market. The historic Minchmoor Road is an ancient right of way dating back at least to medieval times and probably earlier, and is now part of a network of tracks that includes the Southern Upland Way long distance route, winding towards Cockburnspath in the east. It's a stiff challenge for anybody wanting to get close to the wilderness but is nothing like as popular as its northerly cousin the West Highland Way. The scenery, however, is no less appealing in its own way.

ROUTE The collarwork has to be tackled early on in this walk. Opposite the phone box in Yarrowford, on the A708, look for a right of way sign opposite, pointing to the Minchmoor Road. Leave the village where a track rises up into trees, to the right of some wooden garages. A second right of way sign points the way up to a gate. Enter a field and turn left, by a wall, continuing to reach open moorland. The ridge line is now your guide as you head towards Brown Knowe, with the Gruntly Burn separating this ridge from Whitehope Rig on the right. The track traverses Brown Knowe summit on its left to join the Southern Upland Way. At a prominent signpost turn right and follow the way along an old drove road to the top of Brown Knowe. Carry straight on, dropping down to a col.

Stay with the Upland Way as it doglegs between an unnamed top and Broomy Law. Contine on over a path junction to where a ladder stile over the wall on the right marks our eventual descent. For now, though, head towards a forestry plantation and walk along the track to its right, with the Three Brethren visible on the skyline.

Enjoy the expansive view at the summit then return to the ladder stile, this time crossing it. Make your way quite steeply down, passing to the left of a stand of trees further on, to arrive at a bridge taking the road over Yarrow Water. Turn right to get back to the phone box.

Three Brethren

Brown Knowe

Newark Castle

Yarrowford

MAP	OS Sheet 73, Peebles, Galashiels & Selkirk
DISTANCE	9 miles (14km)
RATING	Strenuous. Hill paths
GEAR	Full hill-walking kit

26

MEALL AN T-SEALLAIDH

Rob Roy Macgregor is one of those characters from Scottish history whose very name stirs the blood and has the patriots reaching for their broadswords.

THEMES Outlaw, renegade, rustler or do-gooder, call him what you will, the name of Rob Roy Macgregor resonates throughout Scottish history. He and his wife are laid to rest right at the foot of this hill in a grave at Balquhidder kirkyard. Go and pay your respects before you set out, for whatever anyone thinks of Rob Roy he certainly had the ability to lead and command respect from his people, and deserves admiration for that alone. Several scenes stand out in my mind from the 1995 film starring Liam Neeson as the eponymous hero – but one is more memorable than the rest. Dishevelled, bruised and humiliated, Macgregor suddenly sees his chance to escape his English captors and jumps over the side of a bridge. He is cut free to prevent him strangling the vile Archibald Cunningham, to whom he's tied, and runs off down the bed of a burn with soldiers in hot pursuit, leaving Cunningham with a very sore neck.

To shake them off Macgregor hides inside the stinking carcass of a Highland cow – typical of the guile to which he must have resorted

time and again. Cunningham justly gets his come-uppance in the end, of course, when he's killed by Macgregor in a duel.

ROUTE Balquhidder village is a peaceful place, set in lovely countryside, and a fitting location for the hero to be entombed. Follow the path behind the kirk leading north into forestry in Kirkton Glen and eventually Glen Dochart, with the A85 running through it giving access to Crianlarich and eventually Rannoch Moor and Glencoe. Our route, however, goes only as far as Lochan an Eireannaich. Now ascend Meall an Fiodhain and continue south-east along the ridge to the top of Cam Chreag. Avoid crags on the south side of this by descending east and turning them to come back south and on towards the summit of Meall an t-Seallaidh, a Corbett at 852m, where there is a trig point and a good view. Leave the top to head along the south ridge until it is possible to get back to the forestry track and then Balquhidder.

Carn Chreag

Meall an t-Seallaidh

Kirkton Glen

Loch Voil

Balquhidder

MAP	OS Sheet 51, Loch Tay
DISTANCE	7 miles (11km)
RATING	Strenuous. Mountain paths
GEAR	Full hill-walking kit

27

HILL OF CAT

Cats are wandering creatures by nature, and their stravaiging is reflected in the frequency with which they crop up in the names of hills and landscape features.

THEMES On the border between England and Wales stands a favourite little ridge of mine called The Cat's Back, and in the Lake District there's Catbells, of course. In Scotland, the Lochan nan Cat below Perthshire's Ben Lawers clearly derives its name from its shape – just like a feline creature when viewed from above. And here's another border hill for our walk, again with a feline nomenclature, dividing Angus from Deeside. Hill of Cat is reached from the hamlet of Tarfside along two ancient hill highways, the Fungle and Firmount roads, dating back to the 13th century. Their former status as trade routes, joining places, and well trodden by drovers, makes them designated rights of way, most useful for modern wanderers among the hills. The little hamlet of Tarfside holds special significance for me, since it figured as a haven on two walks across Scotland I undertook in the 1980s. At the Parsonage a warm welcome awaited walkers taking part in the Ultimate Challenge. There was endless tea and cakes, and everyone was made to feel perfectly at home as we swapped stories of our routes and engaged in the friendly banter that unites those who love the countryside.

ROUTE From Tarfside, head north along a track just before a bridge crossing the Water of Tarf. A Scottish Rights of Way sign marks the route. Follow the track across open moorland, and after crossing a bridge over the Burn of Tennet, a track junction is reached. Bear left, taking the Fungle Road to the cottage at Shinfur. Skirt round the cottage and down to cross the Burn of Clearach, then up the ridge ahead towards Tampie summit, parting company with the Fungle Road to join the Firmounth Road. Descend north from Tampie, still on the Firmounth, to a marshy bealach. Hill of Cat lies to the left. Cross broken ground and follow the line of fence posts to the top of the hill. The posts are a useful navigational aid if mist is enveloping these moors, when the compass becomes a trusty friend. If the summit is clear, Scotland's most easterly Munro, Mount Keen, can be seen almost due west; the Corbett of Mount Battock is prominent to the south-east. Descend south over Hill of Corn, with the wonderfully named Burn of Adedazzle on the right, to reach a good track. Turn left along it to meet the Water of Tarf. Ford this at a convenient point and carry on past Baillies and then Burnfoot further on. Cross a bridge over the burn, returning to Tarfside.

Hill of Cat

Glentennet

Water of Tarf

Baillies

Glen Esk

Tarfside

MAP	OS Sheet 44, Ballater
DISTANCE	11 miles (17km)
RATING	Strenuous. Tracks and paths
GEAR	Full hill-walking kit

28

GLEOURAICH & SPIDEAN MIALACH

Gaelic names can be notoriously difficult to pronounce for non-speakers, but at least one of these peaks has a nickname to make it easier – 'Spider on ma leg'

THEMES Stalking is an activity vital to the economy of many Highland estates, and while shooting deer might not sit well with the sensitivities of animal lovers, it keeps a lot of people in work and maintains the environment in a healthy state. One of the benefits for walkers of this historically well-established pursuit is the network of stalking tracks that seam the estates. These old stalking tracks, which blend in perfectly with the surroundings, provide good, well-drained surfaces on which to tread. They also take the easiest lines up hills, and that's just the case on these two, with a path getting well up towards the summit of the first. Then it's an exhilarating ridge walk to the second, 'Spider on ma leg', before the descent. I experienced one of the most dramatic sights I've ever seen in the Highlands on Gairich, a Munro south of Loch Quoich some years ago. It was an incredible temperature inversion where my walking companion and I broke through the cloud layer on top of the hill to witness the most eerie and beautiful scene, with a carpet of cloud and peaks sticking above it everywhere. Getting to the start of the walk on the shores of Loch Quoich involves a bit of a tortuous

drive, but the scenery is wonderful and there is the added advantage of the Tomdoun Hotel en route – a good watering hole to spend the night before driving on to the loch, unless you want to camp closer.

ROUTE Leaving Fort William, take the Road to the Isles, which heads towards Kyle of Lochalsh and the Skye bridge. Just over two miles past the start of Loch Garry, a minor road cuts left, following the loch side on to the Tomdoun, then snaking its way to Loch Quoich. On reaching the loch, drive on for about two and a half miles to a little bridge over the Allt Coire Peitireach. The stalking path is on the left bank of the burn, marked by a cairn. Follow it all the way up Gleoraich's south ridge and then on to the top. A series of spectacular, steep corries now become evident, scooped out of the northern faces of the two hills. Marvel at them as you continue east, with a fair drop in height before reaching Spidean Mialach. Carry on east past the summit to reach a spur leading down to Loch Fearna, which can be seen below. From the edge of the loch go west to pick up another stalker's path that leads back almost to the start.

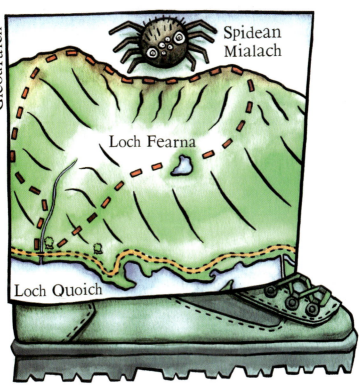

Gleouraich

Spidean Mialach

Loch Fearna

Loch Quoich

MAP	OS Sheet 33, Loch Alsh & Glen Shiel
DISTANCE	6 miles (10km)
RATING	Strenuous. Mountain paths
GEAR	Full hill-walking kit

29

LOCH EILDE MOR

With so much rainfall, it's hardly surprising that Scotland's landscape is peppered with lochs and reservoirs, and they provide interesting goals for walkers.

THEMES Just like its giant neighbour, the Blackwater Reservoir on Rannoch Moor, Loch Eilde Mor is readily accessible only to those willing to do some legwork. Its Gaelic name translates as "Big Loch of the Hind", and it can be reached from Kinlochleven. It could be argued that walkers have saved Kinlochleven's economic bacon since the creation of the West Highland Way. In other respects, the place has been dealt a poor hand. Construction of the Ballachulish bridge, which opened in 1975, spared motorists the long drive around Loch Leven or a queue for the ferry. But Kinlochleven lost some tourist trade. Then in 2000 came the demise of the big aluminium smelter, which had provided employment since the arrival of the British Aluminium Company in 1904. The annual stream of WHW walkers, who seek provisions and overnight stops before the final push to Fort William, has helped to redress the balance, as have initiatives such as the visitor centre that tells the story of aluminium smelting, and now even an indoor ice climbing wall.

ROUTE Take the road from Glencoe village to Kinlochleven and locate St Paul's Church in Kinlochmore. A public car park is provided nearby. Exit the car park, turning right past the church. Carry on to the B863 and turn right over a bridge crossing the Allt Coire na Ba, heading along the road to a West Highland Way marker. Follow the WHW up through woodland to a point where the path emerges on to open moorland, crossing a minor road in the process. Further on it joins a track at another WHW marker. Leave the Way, and turn right along the track. It skirts the hillside to Mamore Lodge. Carry straight on past the lodge, following a footpath round a house to rejoin the track. Continue north along the Allt Coire na Ba with the Mamores towering above. Cross a wooden bridge and bear right. Continue towards Loch Eilde Mor, ignoring a path branching right at the highest point on the track. Follow another path, which rounds the head of the loch to a dam over the Allt na h-Eilde. Cross it and turn right. After the second of two metal huts the path reaches a cairn marking the descent to the River Leven. Head down, passing through trees nearer the bottom. At a gap in a wall, go up to meet another path and turn right. Cross a bridge, and pass through woods back to Kinlochmore. At a fork turn left, then right, heading back to the start.

Loch Eilde Mor

West Highland Way

Blackwater Reservoir

KINLOCHLEVEN

MAP	OS Sheet 41, Ben Nevis
DISTANCE	9 miles (14 km)
RATING	Moderate. Paths and tracks
GEAR	Full hill-walking kit

30

BEINN ALLIGIN

If Michaelangelo had been a sculptor of mountains, he could not have produced a finer work of art than this shapely Torridon beauty.

THEMES It translates from Gaelic as 'jewelled peak', and what a gem it is. Beinn Alligin has a natural symmetry and grandeur that makes walkers desperately want to climb it. Striding out high up on the cirque that forms the traverse provides one of Scotland's classic mountain experiences. Part of the great triumvirate that includes Beinn Eighe and the mighty Liathach, Beinn Alligin rises to a height of 3,232ft. That's relatively modest in Munro terms, but it's not height we are concerned with here, it's quality, with a tingle of excitement to be had crossing the Horns of Alligin. You somehow sense that you are in an ancient landscape, and these mountains are formed from some of the oldest rocks on earth – the distinctive terracotta-coloured Torridonian sandstone, punctuated in places by quartzite, giving the impression of perpetual snow.

Of the Torridon triptych, Beinn Alligin is probably best tackled first by anyone making an inaugural visit. Beinn Eighe demands a longer approach and Liathach is technically more difficult.

ROUTE Start at the car park on the Torridon to Diabaig road near Torridon House, where a bridge crosses the Abhain Coire Mhic Nobuil. A climber's path to the left of the bridge, marked by cairns, heads across the moor into Coir' nan Laogh. Continue to the head of the corrie and climb Tom na Gruagaich, Hill of the Maiden, with superb views. See how many features you can identify, but steer clear of Tom na Gruagaich's steep north-east face, which plunges sheer for hundreds of feet to the moor below. Descend a narrow, rocky ridge north to a col. Beyond this the ridge becomes broader, still with steep drops to the right. It curves around to reach Sgurr Mhor, the summit of this fine Munro. Shortly before the top you'll pass the great gash of the Eag Dhubh – the Black Cleft – which adds greatly to the character of the mountain. From here, those of a nervous disposition can return by the same route, but that would be to miss out on all the fun and an exhilarating continuation that makes for a much more satisfying day. From Sgurr Mhor descend quite steeply to tackle the pinnacles of Na Rathanan – the Horns of Alligin – which involves some scrambling but with little technical difficulty. It is possible to bypass them on a deer path to the right. Continue the descent south-east to the moor, where a stalkers' path leads back to the Coire Mhic Nobuil footpath.

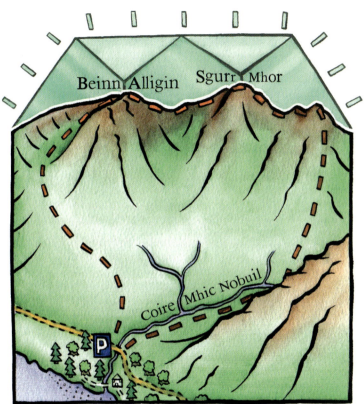

Beinn Alligin Sgurr Mhor

Coire Mhic Nobuil

Loch Torridon Torridon

MAP	OS Outdoor Leisure, Cuillin & Torridon hills
DISTANCE	6 miles (10km)
RATING	Strenuous. Hill paths, some scrambling
GEAR	Full hill-walking kit

31

DUMYAT

At the most westerly end of the Ochils, near Stirling, Dumyat was once populated, and the remains of an Iron Age fort, though difficult to spot, still exist. The name Dumyat is thought to mean 'hill fort of the Maeatae'.

THEMES The Maeatae was a confederation of Pictish tribes opposed to the Roman invasion of this part of Scotland, led by the Emperor Severus around the year 208. Strong evidence of the Roman occupation exists not far away in the Falkirk area, in the form of the Antonine Wall. At not much over 1,300ft, Dumyat nevertheless offers extensive views out over the expansive Carse of Stirling – a flat flood plain extending to the River Forth. The remains of whales have been discovered here, and it's likely that the diet of people who lived on Dumyat in prehistoric times included whale meat. These days, if you venture up Dumyat at the turn of the year you'll have plenty of company. It's become something of a tradition to celebrate the new year with a visit to the top. Shortbread and a dram are more likely fare than whale meat. Standing somewhat aloof from its Ochils neighbours, Dumyat's rocky façade towers over the little settlement of Blairlogie, directly in its shadow, and the town of Menstrie further east. The rock is volcanic and friable, and some years ago a house in Blairlogie paid the price for its proximity to Dumyat when a huge boulder trundled off the hill and crashed through the roof. Fortunately no-one was injured.

ROUTE Take the Sheriffmuir road, which climbs up behind Stirling University and ultimately joins the A9 near Blackford on the north side of the Ochils. No more than a couple of miles along this road from the Stirling side there are some obvious pull-offs on the right. Find a space here – they tend to be busy at times, but there's generally room for all. You'll know you're in the right place if you can see Cocksburn Reservoir away to the left. The chances are you'll have company at some stage during the walk, for this is a well-used route.

Cross a stile on to the moorland and follow your nose due east on a series of obvious paths. The walking is far from strenuous, and you can stroll along enjoying the fresh air and the views. After a time the path bears around to the left, dipping down to cross a boggy area that feeds the burn running down between Dumyat's two tops. The path bears right again to curve round under the summit. A final short scramble lands you on the top where, especially on new year's day, you can join the cheerful throng of sundry other adults, children and dogs. Return by the same route.

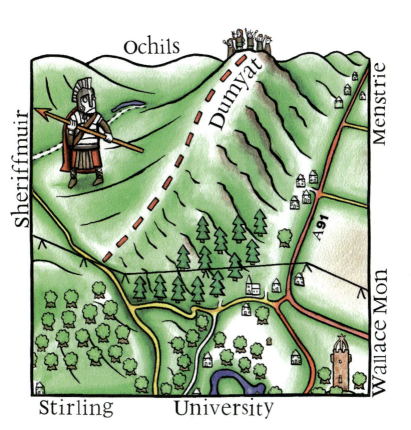

Ochils

Dumyat

Sheriffmuir

Menstrie

A91

Wallace Mon

Stirling

University

MAP	OS Sheet 57, Stirling and Trossachs, or Harveys Superwalker Ochil Hills
DISTANCE	3.5 miles (8km)
RATING	Easy. Hill paths
GEAR	Full hill-walking kit

32

FALLS OF ROGIE

Well-heeled Victorians conscious of their health frequented the spa towns to 'take the waters' with their renowned restorative powers.

THEMES They are commonplace all over Britain now – resorts where you can take a luxury break and pamper yourself with anything from a massage to a mudbath. In Victorian times, the spa towns became popular destinations, where the moneyed classes went to sample waters from natural springs. Strathpeffer was one such place in the Highlands which bore the distinction of offering the world's first peat bath. It was landowner Anne Hay-Mackenzie, Countess of Cromartie and Duchess of Sutherland, who supported the development of Strathpeffer as a spa town. Between 1907 and 1927 the spa was run by a syndicate of Harley Street doctors, who prescribed drinking or bathing in the waters from five local wells for a variety of ailments. In the 1920s, a sulphur bath, said to ease aching limbs and help cure rheumatic pain, cost 2s 6d (15p), while 9s (45p) would buy you a peat bath that could supposedly help with arthritis or even with obesity.

ROUTE From the centre of Strathpeffer, take the A834 towards Jamestown. At the edge of the town follow the route signposted to Garve. At a bend turn left, making for Loch Kinellan. Walk round the left-hand shore of the loch and keep straight on along an indistinct path to the edge of a plantation. Follow the forest track to a signpost and turn left towards View Rock, following green waymarkers. At View Rock a spur path leads to the viewpoint. Next comes a steep descent. Stick with green waymarkers downhill to a forest road. Turn left, then right to a path on the left. Cross over a forest road to a car park. On its far side, look for a River Walk sign. Pass a culvert and follow the path right to a forest road. Turn left, signposted Garve, then bear left downhill. A track on the left is signed to Falls of Rogie. Cross a footbridge below the falls and turn right, following green waymarkers. The path turns west, away from the river, and traverses rocky terrain to a junction. Turn right to reach a car park. Leave it through a wooden arch and return to the falls. Retrace your outward route, but instead of continuing to the car park, bear sharp left up a forest road towards Loch na Crann. At a four-way junction, turn right between boulders on to a track. Cut off left to rejoin the track higher up. Continue to the far end of Loch Kinellan. Turn left along a lane, which becomes a track. Go through a gate to the left of a house and carry on into trees, with a signpost for Strathpeffer.

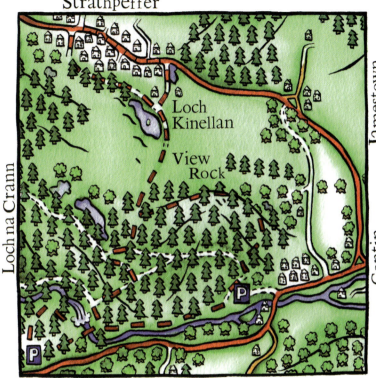

Strathpeffer

Loch
Kinellan

View
Rock

Loch na Crann

Jamestown

Contin

Rogie Falls

MAP	OS Sheet 26, Inverness and Strathglass
DISTANCE	10 miles (16km)
RATING	Moderate. Waymarked paths and tracks
GEAR	Full hill-walking kit

33

BEN TIRRAN

Hardy walkers naturally gravitate to the giant peaks of the Grampians, but there's plenty of wonderful countryside to wander in further east, among the Angus glens.

THEMES Walking coast-to-coast across Scotland, as I have done several times, is an uplifting experience that keeps you in touch with the landscape for days on end. Leaving the Grampians behind, the gentle Angus glens act like a filter, channelling you towards the coast and the seaside towns of the east – Montrose prominent amongst them. There is ample wild countryside here in which to stretch the legs, as a study of the map will reveal. Follow Jock's Road, the right of way that leads through the hills from near the royal territory of Braemar, and you funnel down into Glen Clova. A long, meandering glen, it provides ready access to wide open spaces. There are Munros to be tackled, but those who come for them alone and ignore everything else are much the poorer. This circuit takes in the fine Corbett of Ben Tirran and two sparkling lochs. Hidden from view down in the glen, they sit at the base of 'hanging corries' – Nature's legacy of a glacial past.

ROUTE Start from the car park at Clova, the small hamlet high up the glen. A path to the right of the Clova Hotel, a friendly hostelry handy for refreshments at the end of the

walk, rises fairly steeply and before long divides. Take the left branch and continue upwards towards Loch Brandy. At a height of over 2,000ft it's a real gem, and a great place to just sit and contemplate, with cliffs rising behind. It's also home to a tiny and very rare water creature known as the diatom - a vivid orange colour. Gird your loins and press on, ascending the ridge known as the Snub to reach Green Hill. This opens up a real panorama of the surrounding hill country, with peak upon peak in sight. Head eastwards across the grassy plateau to Ben Tirran, keeping an eye out for the birds that inhabit Scotland's high moorland areas – curlew, ptarmigan, skylarks singing as they rise and, if you're lucky, the shy dotterel. From the summit head south west, then down to Loch Wharral – almost a mirror image in form to Loch Brandy, but smaller. Take the path heading down and left of the loch outflow. It joins a track. Continue descending close to the burn. Just before a plantation turn right to cross the burn and head down along the edge of the trees. At the foot of the hill go through another gate on to the road. Amble gently along the last two miles to the car park at the start.

MAP	OS Sheet 44, Glen Clova
DISTANCE	10 miles (16km)
RATING	Strenuous. Mountain paths
GEAR	Full hill-walking kit

34

FLOWERDALE WATERFALL

Watching whales and dolphins might not be immediately linked to Scotland, but it is possible to see them off the Scottish coast if you know where to go.

THEMES It sounds more like a dramatic extract from Moby Dick than something that could have happened in a Scottish sea loch. The three fishermen out on Loch Ewe in 1809 would hardly have been expecting an encounter with a leviathan of the deep, but their boat was battered and sunk by one and they were drowned. If you want to have a chance of seeing whales, dolphins and porpoises in Scottish waters, this is the place to do it, with the Gulf Stream bringing in its food-rich waters that attract them. A little patience is needed, but sightings are always a thrilling experience and not unusual. The Gairloch Marine Life Centre runs cruises, but it is also possible to see these elegant creatures from the shore. Whaling in Scotland – once a thriving industry in places such as Shetland – ended in 1951. The museum in Lerwick has an informative display on whaling in Shetland. The practice is still prevalent in other parts of the world and arouses strong emotions among conservationists and its proponents in the whaling nations. The University of St Andrews is one of those at the forefront of research into ways of preventing dolphins and porpoises getting caught in fishing nets and killed.

ROUTE Once you're done with dolphin watching after an early start, head off from the car park alongside the A832 on the southern shore of Gairloch at Charlestown. Make for Flowerdale House. Go past this, following red-topped waymarker poles. Follow the path left of the burn and on to a footbridge built by the Royal Engineers, then to Flowerdale Waterfall. It's worth the detour along a rough path to the little hill of An Groban for the view.

Return to the bridge and go past the waterfall to cross another bridge and head back, now on the other side of the burn. At a concrete bridge turn left, through felled trees, to reach a blue-topped waymarker and another footbridge. Follow the blue-topped poles, making a right turn back towards Flowerdale Mains. Continue meandering back through trees to the Old Inn at Charlestown – a fine watering hole that serves food. Go down towards the pier. Follow a tarmac path signposted to the beach. It emerges from a pinewood and turns sharp right for the fort of An Dun. Continue around the shore to arrive at the car park.

Gairloch

Charlestown

An Groban

MAP	OS Sheet 72, Gairloch and Ullapool
DISTANCE	5 miles (8km)
RATING	Moderate. Track and paths, mostly waymarked
GEAR	Boots and a waterproof

35

CAIRNSMORE OF FLEET

The start of this walk is remarkable for the presence of one of the most unusual signs you're likely to see anywhere – 'Take care, red squirrels crossing', and there's a good chance you'll see one too.

THEMES There's no doubt that red squirrels have that 'cuddly creature' factor that makes us all warm to them. They are more secretive than the ubiquitous greys, so a walk where there's a fair likelihood of seeing one, right at the start, has to be high on the agenda. There are two other hills in the region which share Cairnsmore as part of their names – Cairnsmore of Carsphairn, the highest of the three, and Cairnsmore, or Black Craig of Dee. Cairnsmore of Fleet is by far the most popular, however, with a tremendous view from its summit. Just before the top is reached, an oblong granite block is passed with a number of names inscribed on it. It stands testimony to the airmen who died in no fewer than eight plane crashes during the war years, between 1940 and 1944. Canadians, New Zealanders and Dutch crew, as well as Britons, all lost their lives. Two US airforce pilots are also commemorated, killed when their Phantom jet crashed in 1979. But let's not be morbid, for this is a lovely walk, and in a part of Scotland that remains largely undiscovered for those who pass it by for the better known haunts further north. Spend some time here and you'll be well rewarded.

ROUTE The start can be a little tricky to find for those unfamiliar with the area. On the A75 heading for Stranraer, about three miles before Newton Stewart, look out for a prominent white farmhouse on the right at GR457629. Turn right on to the road that passes this, which becomes a rough track. Drive on to reach a viaduct. Cross this and turn immediately right through a metal gate into Cairnsmore Estate. Follow the track to a white building facing you and go left around it to reach the small car parking area next to Cairnsmore Farm. Go through the gate on the far side of the car park and head diagonally across a field to the top left hand corner, where there is a metal gate, hidden until you get close to it. Carry on along a rather muddy path through a small broadleaf plantation into a much larger forest of pines. An obvious path cuts a swathe uphill. Emerge from the forest and cross a stile to continue upwards more steeply. The path zig-zags on, eventually levelling off before the summit. Take care on the last section in mist, because the moorland is featureless here. A compass bearing is advised to avoid wandering off route. In clear weather there's no problem. Return by the same line.

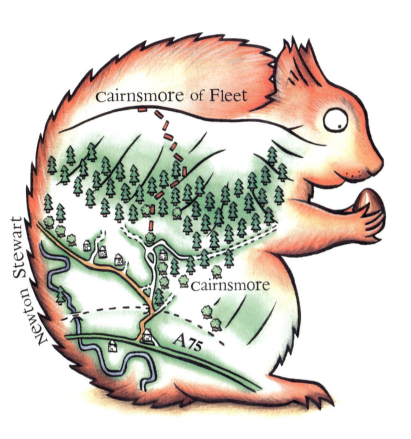

Cairnsmore of Fleet

Newton Stewart

Cairnsmore

A 75

MAP	OS Sheet 83, Newton Stewart and Kirkcudbright
DISTANCE	6 miles (10km)
RATING	Moderate. Forest and hill path
GEAR	Full hill-walking kit

36

CLACHNABEN

Tors and outcrops give hills a distinctive character that makes them easily recognisable. Two stand out in the north east.

THEMES The old favourite of Bennachie, beloved friend of many, has its granite crown – the Mither Tap. Another popular objective for walkers is Clachnaben, which attracts upwards of 15,000 visitors a year. They are drawn to its granite eminence rising prominently from the summit to around 100ft. An unfortunate corollary of popularity is erosion. Fortunately Clachnaben has benefited from some commendable path repairs thanks to the Clachnaben Trust. Inspired by a similar group of committed conservationists – the Baillies of Bennachie – the Trust succeeded in dealing with the erosion through a programme of phased works, engaging professional path repairers, helped by volunteers. Funds came from Scottish Natural Heritage grants totalling £120,000, together with contributions from the Mountaineering Council of Scotland, hill walking groups and other sources. It is really great to see walkers giving something back to the environment in which they seek enjoyment. If the funds can be raised it means the environment and walkers alike reap the rewards.

ROUTE From the car park north of Glendye Lodge, just off the B974 Fettercairn to Banchory road, take the wide path through trees to emerge on a track. Turn left and continue down to a bridge across a burn. At a track junction turn right and follow the burn upstream to cross an area of moorland called Miller's Bog. At another track junction half a mile or so from the bridge, go straight on to a gate on the edge of a forestry plantation. Skirt the woodland on its left, staying with the burn. At the top edge of the woodland climb up to the col between Clachnaben and neighbouring Mount Shade.

Carry on up to the summit of Clachnaben, on your left, with its granite tor. Scramble on to the top for a panoramic view. From Clachnaben summit take the obvious path west to the top of Hill of Edendocher, where there's a cluster of posts.

Turn left along a good track towards a prominent cairn on the shoulder of the hill. The track descends to the lower top of Cairn of Finglenny. Carry on down beside the Brocky Burn into Glen Dye and a cottage at Charr. Turn east to walk down through Glen Dye. At a track junction further on, ignore the right branch and continue straight on to skirt round Netty Hill. Keep on the same forward line to reach the bridge crossed near Glendye Lodge on the outward route, and head back to the car park.

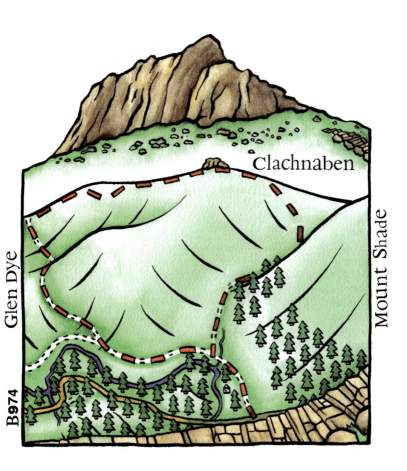

Clachnaben

Glen Dye

B974

Mount Shade

MAP	OS Sheet 45, Stonehaven
DISTANCE	10 miles (16km)
RATING	Strenuous. Hill paths
GEAR	Full hill-walking kit

37

BEN CRUACHAN

James Bond movie buffs will be familiar with the scene: caverns and tunnels full of intriguing, colourful pipework and machinery suggesting that something sinister is going on underground, with the promise that action is in store.

THEMES Visit the Cruachan hydro scheme and you are not likely to get shot at or blown up, but it's not difficult to let your imagination run wild. Unlike a movie set, though, there is a practical purpose to it all – the production of electricity to provide light, heat homes and drive computers. It's an amazing technical achievement and ranks as the world's first pumped storage scheme, now run by Scottish Power. No doubt a similar proposal today would run into environmental opposition to the creation of a giant dam cradled in a high mountain corrie. The reservoir, created in 1965, is an essential part of the plant's operation. The principle is a bit like a giant battery. Deep underground, the huge reversible turbines use low-cost electricity at night to pump water from Loch Awe up to the reservoir. That, together with water collected from the natural run-off on the mountain slopes, thunders down during the day to drive the turbines and meet peak demand for electricity.

ROUTE Start from the roadside near the power station on the A85 Dalmally to Oban road. Parking in the power station car park is frowned upon, so use a layby on the road. Go under the railway, picking up the path on the west side of the Cruachan burn, climbing steeply through oak, birch and hazel woods. It's also possible to ascend on the east side of the burn to the Cruachan dam, but the west path gives access more quickly to the grassy slopes of Meall Cuanail – the ultimate objective whichever route is taken. Once on the summit, the drop is a mere couple of hundred feet before the climb up to Ben Cruachan. Head up Cruachan's south ridge, which is littered with granite boulders. A faint path weaves through them to reach the sharp summit and a majestic view on a clear day. In bad visibility, care is needed with navigation, especially from here on. There now follows some excellent high-level ridge walking as we progress to the next top, Drochaid Glas – actually on a spur north of the main ridge line. A little mild scrambling is involved, but nothing desperate. Back on the ridge, the prize of another Munro awaits in the shape of Stob Diamh. To complete the horseshoe, turn south for the peak of Stob Garbh. Carry on to a bealach, and thence down to the south-east corner of the reservoir before the final descent back to the roadside.

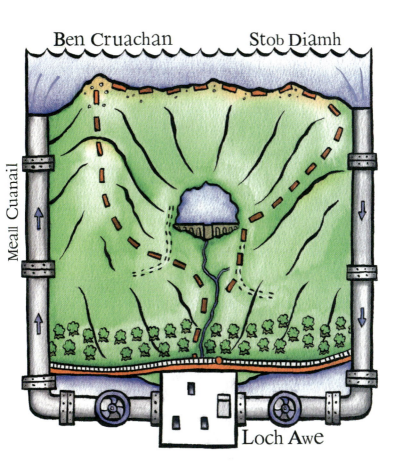

Ben Cruachan

Stob Diamh

Meall Cuanail

Loch Awe

MAP	OS Sheet 50, Glen Orchy
DISTANCE	7.5 miles (12 km)
RATING	Strenuous. Mountain paths
GEAR	Full hill-walking kit

38

LURCHER'S CRAG

With the Cairngorms established as the second national park to be created in Scotland, this walk gives a flavour of the spectacular northern corries.

THEMES The Cairngorms are the closest Britain gets to an arctic climate and landscape. Just a few degrees colder in winter and glaciers would be a distinct possibility – not that it's likely to happen with the effects of global warming. The evidence of past glacial activity is obvious here, and there's an abundance of cold-climate wildlife: ptarmigan and hares whose coats turn pure white in winter, reindeer, and even snowy owls. The northern corries are a winter climber's paradise, providing excellent and challenging sport when conditions are right. But you don't have to be a climber to enjoy the majesty of this place. On a crisp winter's day when the frost has bitten hard, the sun picks out the pristine snow crystals. In fact, a visit in any season will reap rewards. But keep a wary eye out, if the mist is down, for The Big Grey Man, who is said to stalk the plateau.

ROUTE Start from the car park under Cairn Gorm, now with its funicular railway. In winter you'll be mingling with skiers. At other times the area is the preserve of tourists and walkers. Cross the bridge in the top corner of the car park that gives access to the path leading round to Coire

an Sneachda and Coire an Lochain. This path has had a lot of professional restoration work carried out on it, and is well drained and firm. Even the sections that used to be boggy have been taken care of. Continue along the path, skirting Coire an Sneachda, the first corrie you come to, and head on, climbing gently all the way, towards Coire an Lochain. The mouth of the corrie gives a view of the cliffs that rise above the lochan, and the very distinctive feature of a massive rock slab which gets covered by snow in winter and is prone to avalanche. Don't walk into the corrie but head on up the ridge to its right, making for a flattish area of ground on the horizon between Cairn Lochan and Lurcher's Crag. Once at this bealach, bear round to the right and scramble up through the boulders to reach the rocky summit. You've climbed to 1,053 metres – higher than Munro height, but you're not on a Munro. The view, however, is mind-boggling, with a precipitous drop into the deep defile of the Lairig Ghru – the great pass that splits the Cairngorms. Return by the same route or, for the more adventurous, there are endless possibilities – perhaps a circuit over Cairn Lochan and down through Coire an Sneachda, or even round to Cairn Gorm.

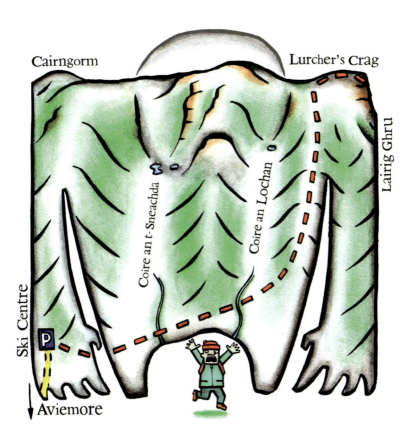

Cairngorm

Lurcher's Crag

Lairig Ghru

Coire an t-Sneachda

Coire an Lochan

Ski Centre

P

Aviemore

MAP	OS Sheet 36, Grantown, Aviemore and Cairngorm area
DISTANCE	5 miles (8km)
RATING	Moderate. Mountain paths
GEAR	Full hill-walking kit

39

SGURR A' CHAORACHAIN

Religion figures prominently in this attractive corner of Scotland, through the work of an Irish monk who established a monastery here and spread the Christian gospel.

THEMES Exploring hidden corners of Scotland is one of the delights of walking, and Applecross is a great place for it, with corries to wander in and out of and steep cliffs to gaze at. As with many parts of the Highlands, the Applecross peninsula has suffered a serious population decline over the years. In 1850 around 3,000 people lived in its scattered townships, thriving on crofting and fishing. Now there are less than a tenth of that number. The traditional means of earning a living are still there, along with tourism. The area was one of the earliest Christian settlements in Scotland, founded by Irish monk Maelrubha in the year 673. For almost 60 years he ran his monastery, and using Applecross as his base spread the gospel to Lochcarron and into Easter Ross. Almost all traces of the settlement have since disappeared, and Clachan Church now stands on the site. Two of the most famous names in climbing – Chris Bonington and Tom Patey – are associated with this hill. They partnered each other on the first ascent of The Cioch Nose, which goes more or less straight up the front of Sgurr a' Chaorachain. In terms of climbing grades it is modest in technical difficulty, but provides spectacular situations and exposure.

ROUTE Start from the bridge over the Russell Burn on the steep, winding road that crosses the Bealach na Ba, the Pass of the Cattle. Follow the burn on its right- hand side heading for Loch Coire nan Arr, from which it issues. There's an impressive view here of the ancient Torridonian sandstone cliffs and the Beinn Bhan massif rising on the right, its complex series of corries hidden from this angle but well worth exploring on another day. Turn left around the head of the loch and make for the horseshoe-shaped corrie facing you, with the ground rising steeply at first and then relenting somewhat. A tiny lochan is reached, and it's time for a breather before the final push to the top of the hill. It's a steep pull over the grass and rocks above – on your left facing the back of the corrie – to reach the grassy col on the ridge below the summit. Turn left and it's soon gained. Enjoy the view, then descend the broad ridge ahead, east and south-east. It steepens, but don't be daunted. Continue carefully south-east, picking your way down over the broken ground until the going gets easier and you arrive at the road leading back to Russell Bridge.

Sgurr a' Chaorachain

Beinn Bhan

Loch Kishorn

Lochcarron

MAP	OS Sheet 24, Raasay and Loch Torridon
DISTANCE	3.5 miles (5km)
RATING	Moderate. Hill paths
GEAR	Full hill-walking kit

40

DOUNE PONDS AND CASTLE

Visit the castle used in the filming of Monty Python and the Holy Grail, and a nature reserve created from old gravel pits.

THEMES The zany humour of the Pythons is well known, and none could do it better. Doune Castle, near Stirling, took on numerous guises in the film as Camelot, the Castle of Guy de Lombard, Swamp Castle and Castle Anthrax. The connection with the movie has helped to boost visitor numbers.

After the Battle of Falkirk in 1746, prisoners taken by the Jacobites were held at Doune. They included the young Reverend John Witherspoon, who later emigrated to America and became one of the architects of the Declaration of Independence. Our walk starts at Doune Ponds – a series of old gravel pits that have been flooded and turned into a nature reserve. It's the perfect environment for a variety of birds.

ROUTE To reach the car park at the ponds, turn off the main street in Doune past Kilmadock's Church. Facing the church, it's the road on the left. Enter the reserve and walk to the main pond. Turn left and follow the path round past two hides. Bear left along a rougher path through trees, parallel to the backs of houses. Descend steps on the right and continue to a clearing,

just after a seat. Go left round some fenced woodland to a flight of steps up a steep banking. Ascend these and turn right at the top along a farm track. Look for a sign saying 'Commonty Walk' at the edge of a beech wood. Follow this walk to reach a road and turn right. After about 50 yards, turn left on to the Doune Trail and continue to some steps on the right. They lead down to an old railway trackbed, once used by trains heading for Oban. Turn right and carry on to a short flight of steps just after a bridge over a minor road. Continue alongside a playing field and on to Doune's main street. Turn left here and follow the road down to the castle entrance. Take the track to the left of the castle ramparts and walk ahead, rounding a small sewage works on its left. Continue to where the Ardoch Burn flows into the River Teith and turn right along a grassy path back towards the castle.

Go round to the left of the castle up a bank to the car park. Leave this on its left hand side and turn left along a track to a gate. Go through it and at a path division bear right along the edge of a fenced field. Turn right through a gate to enter a housing estate and follow your nose to the main street and back to Doune Ponds.

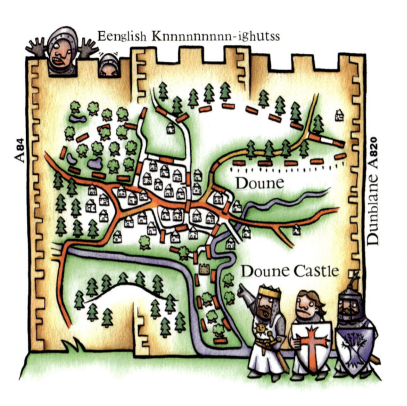

MAP	OS Sheet 57, Stirling and Trossachs
DISTANCE	4 miles (6km)
TERRAIN	Easy. Paths and tracks
GEAR	Boots and a waterproof

41

CASTLE TIORAM

From the wilds of Moidart, on Scotland's rugged west coast, comes a tale to put the fear of God into any thief – and especially a female one.

THEMES At the height of clan rule in Scotland, justice was meted out in a rather more summary fashion than it is these days, within the strictures of a modern legal system. It was about 300 years ago that a girl known as James's daughter was accused, along with male accomplices, of stealing silver from Castle Tioram – an impressive ruin perched on a small islet in Loch Moidart. The castle is reached by a causeway, which floods when the tide is high. The girl's accusers, showing no mercy, took her to the north side of the castle and tied her by the hair, where she was left to drown as the water level rose.

Her partners in crime fared little better, though their deaths were rather more swift. They were hanged from a gallows in sight of the castle. Whether the theft was down to them or others, 200 years later a hoard of silver coins was found below the Silver Walk, close to where the girl was drowned. Laid to siege many times, Castle Tioram was deliberately set on fire in 1715 on the orders of its owner. Allan 'The Red' MacDonald, 14th chief and captain of Clanranald, did not want the fortress falling into Hanoverian hands after he

had left it to fight for the Jacobite cause. Ardnamurchan is a stunningly beautiful area, though full enjoyment of a visit is weather dependent and the prevailing westerly winds often bring rain.

ROUTE The easiest way to reach Loch Moidart is via the Corran Ferry across to the Ardnamurchan Peninsula. Once on the peninsula follow the A861 through Strontian and Salen. About a mile north of the little hamlet of Acharacle, after crossing the River Shiel, a road branches left to reach the loch.

If you are new to Ardnamurchan be prepared, because the terrain can be pathless and rough, so brush up on the navigation and take a good pair of gaiters! Visit Castle Tioram first if the tide is out when you get there. From the car park, walk back along the road to a house. On its right is a stile. Cross this into a field then follow a track, climbing up the hillside alongside a metal water pipe. Go past a lochan on the right and on to the edge of another, where a path branches left. Follow this down towards Loch Moidart, under Beinn Bhreac on your right. The path winds down into woodland on the shore of Loch Moidart. Continue to the lochside path and turn left, following the 'Silver Walk' around the shore to the castle.

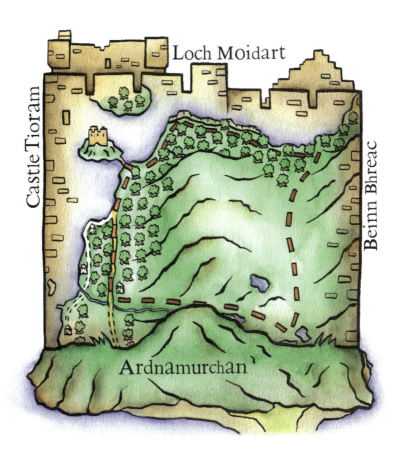

Loch Moidart

Castle Tioram

Beinn Bhreac

Ardnamurchan

MAP	OS Sheet 40, Loch Shiel
DISTANCE	4 miles (6km)
RATING	Easy. Hill paths and tracks
GEAR	Boots and a waterproof

42

BEINN UDLAIDH &
BEN BHREAC-LIATH

Follow in the footsteps of the Robbie Burns of the Gaels, Duncan Ban McIntyre. He was employed as stalker in these parts and based his most famous poem, *In Praise of Beinn Dorain*, on the Munro that towers above the A82 road to Glencoe.

THEMES There was a time when Glen Orchy was much more populous than it is today. In the late 18th century there were at least 10 settlements stretching the 12 miles between Bridge of Orchy and Dalmally. A census conducted by the minister of the parish in 1782 recorded 152 people living there – a total that has dwindled to fewer than a dozen now. Many emigrated to far-flung parts, and there are at least three towns called Glenorchy in other parts of the world. Although extensively planted with conifers, the glen is a place of great scenic grandeur and an excellent venue to pick up a couple of conveniently placed Corbetts – Beinn Udlaidh and Ben Bhreac-liath. A monument to Duncan Ban McIntyre stands near Dalmally. The poet was born in Glen Orchy in 1724. He fought in the battle of Falkirk in January, 1746 on the 'wrong' side, when Bonnie Prince Charlie's 5,000-strong Highland army defeated a much larger force of George II's royal troops. McIntyre survived to gain the favour of the Earl of Breadalbane, who appointed him stalker on the nearby area around Beinn Dorain, where the poet spent 20 years. He must have missed his beloved Highlands

when, in 1767, he and his wife Mairi moved to Edinburgh, where Duncan obtained a position in the Town Guard.

ROUTE Drive down Glen Orchy along the B8074 for about one and a half miles as far as Invergaunan, alongside a forestry plantation. Staying on the edge of the plantation, walk south on the right-hand side of the Allt Ghamhnain, issuing from Coire Ghamhnain above, which divides the two Corbetts on our route. At the top edge of the plantation veer right to climb the ridge up to Beinn Udlaidh's summit, crossing a band of quartzite – the white rock that gives some hills the appearance of having snow on them all year round, Beinn Eighe in Torridon being a distinctive example. The top of Beinn Udlaidh is broad and flat. Turn left to walk east and descend to the wide bealach above Coire Ghamhnain. Keep ahead to tackle the steep slopes of Beinn Bhreac-liath, with the angle easing towards the top. Some pleasant high level ridge walking follows, north towards Glen Orchy again. Where the ridge drops down into the glen, trend left back to Invergaunan to complete the circuit.

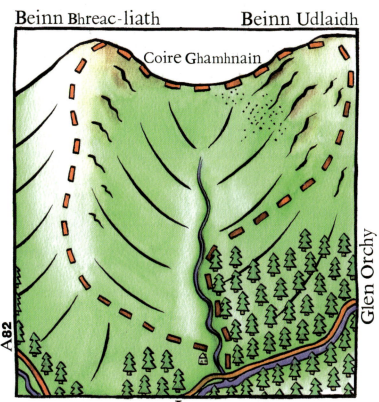

Beinn Bhreac-liath

Beinn Udlaidh

Coire Ghamhnain

Glen Orchy

A82

Invergaunan

MAP	OS Sheet 50, Glen Orchy
DISTANCE	7 miles (11km)
RATING	Moderate. Mountain paths
GEAR	Full hill-walking kit

43

CREAG DHUBH

The hill that shares the battle cry of Clan McPherson is a prominent and shapely landmark for the residents of Newtonmore and Kingussie.

THEMES With a bounty of 11,000 Scots pounds on his head after Culloden, the clan chief of the McPhersons must have been worried that he would be shopped by some unscrupulous countryman keen to get his hands on what, in those days, was a veritable fortune. Still, he managed to evade his pursuers, hiding out in a cave on the slopes of Creag Dhubh for nine years, so the story goes. Cluny's cave is at the western end of this prominent summit, not quite reaching Corbett status but nonetheless impressive for all that, and throwing down quite a challenge to those who would reach the cairn on top. An attractive and photogenic peak, especially from the Newtonmore end, it stands in splendid isolation alongside the A86 Newtonmore to Laggan road. One benefit of this solitude is the views from every point on the summit ridge, which extend for miles in every direction and make the climb well worth the effort. A traverse provides the greatest rewards, but the top can be gained from either end with a descent by the same route. The eastern side provides the easier line, but I'd recommend doing the traverse from the west, walking back towards Newtonmore. It's easier to cope with the necessary scrambling going up.

ROUTE Follow the Laggan road out of Newtonmore for about three miles and look for a lay-by on the right, under the Creag Dhubh crags. It's often used by climbers to gain access to the southern rock face, on which there are numerous routes. Walk along the road a short way to a gate in the fence, just before Creagdhubh Lodge. Go through this gate and follow a path, indistinct in places, that winds its way through woodland fairly steeply up on to the ridge above the crags. Now turn right, being careful to stay well away from the edge of the crags, and cross over a fence on top of a stone dyke. The end of the Creag Dhubh ridge rears up in front. Make for this and follow the path, steep in places and occasionally not very obvious, with some scrambling over rocks required. A better-defined path is eventually reached after a scramble up some slabby rocks, and the route to the top is then obvious, with a final scramble over a shelf to reach the summit, marked with a cairn. From the top continue ahead along the descending ridge where paths appear and disappear. Stick roughly with a middle line until a dip before the next top, Creagan mor. A descent path goes down to the right through birchwoods to arrive at the A86. From here you can walk into Newtonmore.

MAP	OS Sheet 35, Kingussie
DISTANCE	Six miles (10km)
RATING	Strenuous. Hill paths
GEAR	Full hill-walking kit

44

SGURR A' MHAIM

Glen Nevis scythes between the Ben Nevis range and the Grey Corries to the north, and the long chain of the Mamores to the south. It's a happy hunting ground for ridge walkers, with some scrambling added in for those who enjoy it.

THEMES Lording it over every hill in Britain, Scotland's Big Ben has the Carn Mor Dearg arete as a way for scramblers to reach the summit. Its equivalent in the Mamores is the aptly named Devil's Ridge – the link between outlier Sgurr a' Mhaim and the snaking line of the main Mamore chain, which runs west-east. Not for the faint-hearted, it throws down a gauntlet to the walker with a penchant for ridge scrambling. The aspect of Ben Nevis is not very impressive from the glen that shares its name, as it prefers to hide its fearsome cliffs away on the north side. Its distinctive whaleback shape, clear from afar, is not evident here. Pride of place instead goes to Sgurr a' Mhaim, which is nothing like as coy, its huge bulk hitting you smack in the eye as you drive up the glen, hemmed in by peaks on both sides. Visitors sometimes mistake it for Ben Nevis, and in many ways its form makes it more prominent, whereas the Big Ben is more of a complex mass, with many facets.

ROUTE From Fort William drive up Glen Nevis for just over four miles to where the road makes a sharp left turn over the Water of Nevis. Sgurr a' Mhaim rears up on the south side of the bridge. Take the path that follows the left bank of the Allt Coire a' Mhusgain. Break away from this not far along and veer left on to Sgurr a' Mhaim's north-west ridge. It's a pretty relentless climb, assisted higher up by a stalkers' path which zig-zags back and forth. Mercifully the angle eases approaching the top and the rim of a corrie is followed round to the cairn. Those not confident about scrambling can return the same way, still having bagged a Munro. Otherwise carry straight on south and get to grips – literally – with the Devil's Ridge. The scrambling is absorbing and enjoyable, though care is needed, particularly on the most difficult sections near the lowest point. If you're comfortable with scrambling, I'd recommend doing this walk the other way round – anti-clockwise – to avoid the grind up Sgurr a' Mhaim. With the hard scrambling over, continue along the knife-edge crest to Stob Choire a' Mhail. Descend to a broad col and climb rocky ground to the top of another Munro, Sgor an Iubhair, which lies on the main Mamore chain. Descend almost due south to pick up a path that leads west past a small lochan and turns north to follow the All Coire a' Mhisgain back to the start.

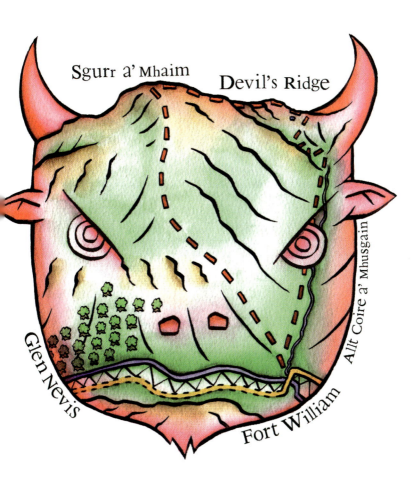

Sgurr a' Mhaim

Devil's Ridge

Glen Nevis

Allt Coire a' Mhusgain

Fort William

MAP	OS Sheet 41, Ben Nevis
DISTANCE	7.5 miles (12km)
RATING	Strenuous. Hill paths, optional scrambling
GEAR	Full hill-walking kit

45

BORERAIG AND SUISNISH

Like the rest of the Highlands and islands, Skye suffered during the mid-19th century from the Clearances, when unscrupulous lairds forced crofters out of their homes.

THEMES The people were cleared off the land to make way for sheep. Some settled elsewhere in Scotland, but many emigrated abroad. The remote hamlets of Boreraig and Suisnish, on the coast of Skye south-west of Broadford, are testimony to that infamous period in Scottish history. If your imagination is strong enough, you can feel the presence of the former inhabitants among the ruins and try to imagine how much they must have suffered.

There were rebellions of course, and further north from here, opposite the southern tip of Raasay, is the Braes, where a famous confrontation over grazing rights occurred in 1882. Known as the Battle of the Braes, the stand-off came about when the sixth Lord MacDonald of Sleat tried to evict tenants, who responded by burning the eviction notices. The sheriff, William Ivory, arrived to arrest the ringleaders with, among others, 50 policemen from Glasgow. The crofters were armed only with sticks and stones and the police arrested five men and injured women during a charge. The men were taken to Inverness and held without trial, but Highlanders from all over Scotland rallied to their cause, standing bail for them and eventually paying their fines. This incident and other skirmishes led

to the Crofters' Holding Act of 1886, giving people security of tenure.

ROUTE Take the A881 south-west from Broadford and drive for about two miles to a ruined church on the right at Cill Chriosd, by Loch Cill Chriosd. Walk back along the road and locate a path on the right. Follow this to reach the course of a former narrow gauge railway and turn right. Continue on the track, passing the remains of a marble quarry, and cross open moorland to where the track rises to its highest point west of Loch Lonachan. Carry on and descend to Boreraig, on the shore of Loch Eishort. The route bears right, following the coastline, past ruined cottages and disused enclosures. Continue along the shore, under the cliffs of Creag an Daraich. Rounding Carn Dearg, the path climbs to the cluster of abandoned buildings at Suisnish, at the entrance to Loch Slapin. A path leads right, back across the moor, but ignore this and turn left to pick up a track that heads north, above the shoreline of Loch Slapin. There are grand views across the loch to Bla Bheinn and the Black Cuillin. Carry on around the bay at Camus Malag to veer inland again and reach the road. Turn right and walk back to the start.

Torrin Skye Broadford

Loch Slapin

Loch Lonachan

Boreraig

Suisnish Loch Eishort

MAP	OS Outdoor Leisure, the Cuillin & Torridon Hills
DISTANCE	10 miles (16km)
RATING	Moderate. Paths, tracks and road
GEAR	Full hill-walking kit

46

BEINN A' CHRULAISTE

The vast expanse of Rannoch Moor is a forbidding yet stunningly wild and beautiful place: the perfect setting for a Sherlock Holmes mystery.

THEMES Looking over the moor from the hills on the south side of Glen Coe always sends a tingle up my spine. It also makes me thankful that I was not among the Scots and Irish labourers who struggled to construct the dam for the lonely Blackwater Reservoir or the grounding for the West Highland Railway, which crosses Rannoch Moor on its way to Fort William. Blackwater dam is more than 3,000ft long and nearly 90ft high, and when constructed formed the largest structure of its kind in Europe. It was built to feed water to a hydro-electric plant that powered the now defunct aluminium smelter at Kinlochleven, and Patrick McGill's book *Children of the Dead End* describes vividly the dreadful conditions endured by the construction workers. Some souls perished in accidents on the site, while others fell victim to the elements and thick mists as they made their way between their work and the Kingshouse Hotel. Many are buried in a graveyard above Kinlochleven, their headstones mere slabs of concrete. The Kingshouse, where they sought refuge in strong drink, was built in the 17th century, and is one of Scotland's oldest licensed inns. After the battle of Culloden it was pressed into service as barracks for George III's troops – hence its name. The soldiers were stationed there to keep unruly Highlanders in check. Dorothy Wordsworth, sister of the poet William, was not impressed when she visited the hostelry, and in 1803 she wrote: "Never did I see such a miserable, wretched place." Things have changed radically for the better, and these days the Kingshouse is friendly and welcoming.

ROUTE At the Kingshouse Hotel, cross the bridge over the River Etive and follow a track that joins the West Highland Way. Cross over the long-distance route and pick up the path beside the Allt a' Bhalaich, issuing from Coire Bhalach at the centre of the cirque of hills ahead. Continue upwards beside the burn and veer off left to climb the broad south-east ridge of Beinn a' Chrulaiste. On reaching the trig pillar at the summit, descend the north ridge, with Blackwater Reservoir constantly in sight as a backdrop. A bealach is reached, from where more uphill work follows to gain the first of Meall Bhalach's twin tops – this one slightly higher than the other. From the second top, descend slopes that are fairly steep to the base of the corrie and pick up the outward route alongside the burn to return to the Kingshouse.

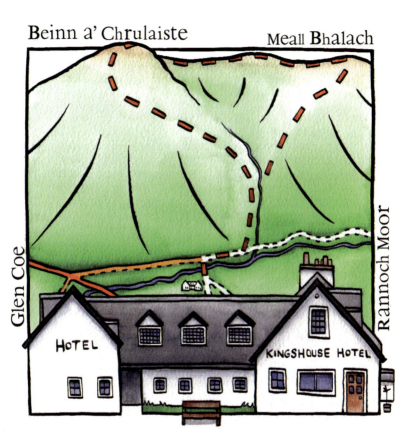

Beinn a' Chrulaiste

Meall Bhalach

Glen Coe

Rannoch Moor

HOTEL

KINGSHOUSE HOTEL

MAP	OS Sheet 41, Ben Nevis
DISTANCE	5.5 miles (9 km)
RATING	Moderate. Hill paths and tracks
GEAR	Full hill-walking kit

47

WANLOCKHEAD

Wanlockhead bears the distinction of being the highest village in Scotland, with an industrial heritage founded on lead – mined as far back as the 13th century.

THEMES As well as lead, gold was also discovered in the area, and was used by the Scottish treasury to make coins in the 1540s. But it was principally lead and zinc that sustained the economy and provided employment until the last mines closed in the 1950s. For walkers interested in industrial history, this outing has a lot to offer, with the museum at Wanlockhead providing all the information you need about life in the area during the period of mining activity. By the 19th century, when it reached a peak, around 850 people lived in the village, and in 1871 the miners founded a co-operative society, buying their supplies through the organisation and sharing the profits. Education was a priority, and in 1756 the minister and a group of villagers established a subscription library, only the second to be set up in Europe. The miners' children learned to read, write and count, and could even take lessons in Latin and Greek.

ROUTE Across the road from Wanlockhead Museum car park is a sign for the Southern Upland Way. Follow the path, passing the remains of Pate's Knowe smelt mill on the left, then New Glencrieff mine – the last to be closed in the late 1950s. An old beam engine on the other side of Wanlock Water, which was formerly used for mine drainage, is the only example that is left in Scotland. Leaving the industrial landscape behind, the path becomes a track. After the Shieling Burn, on the left, cross Wanlock Water on to a good track on the opposite side. Continue along this to reach a girder bridge with a sign for the Southern Upland Way. Follow the track upwards, skirting Glengaber Hill. Continue to the top of a gully where a burn runs down to join Wanlock Water. To the east is the prominent top of Sowen Dod. Turn south to climb Glengaber Hill. Descend and climb again to Shieling Rig, then Stood Hill. The obvious landmark of Lowther Hill can be seen to the south-east, festooned with pylons and the giant 'golf balls' of the Civil Aviation Authority radar station. From Stood Hill summit head down, following a fence to the col below Black Hill. Climb the hill to enjoy a grand view of Wanlockhead. Descend over the broad spur to the road, back to the start.

Glengaber Hill

Stood Hill

Leadhills

Wanlockhead

MAP	OS Sheet 71, Lanark and Upper Nithsdale
DISTANCE	4.5 miles (7km)
RATING	Moderate. Hill paths and tracks
GEAR	Full hill-walking kit

48

TILLICOULTRY TO BLACKFORD

In exceptionally dry weather when the reservoirs are well down, buildings hidden under the water appear again.

THEMES Our need for water led in the past to many farms, and even entire villages, disappearing beneath millions of gallons of the natural resource we all depend on for domestic and commercial life – indeed life itself. In the Lake District, Wales, the Peak District and Scotland, the memories of concealed ghost towns and steadings are revived with drought. In a very dry spell in 2003, the buzz in the Ochils centred on the reappearance of a ruined steading in Upper Glendevon Reservoir at the heart of the hills. It vanished beneath the waters of the new reservoir in the early 1950s. An old trade route passes right through the Ochils from Tillicoultry to Blackford, passing the reservoir. As one of the 'Hillfoot' towns below the steep southern escarpment of the Ochils, Tillicoultry once supported a thriving woollen industry, dating back to the early 16th century. Blackford is best known these days as the home of the bottled water Highland Spring, but is notable historically for having Scotland's first public brewery.

ROUTE From just behind the Woolpack Inn in Tillicoultry Glen, look for the right of way sign along a path that goes up steps, then on to the open hill above the town. Follow the path as it snakes its way along the shoulder of the hill on the right hand side of the glen. The path arrives at a boggy area under King's Seat hill. Now head almost due north, keeping to the right of Andrew Gannel Hill and making for Skythorn Hill. The path can be difficult to follow here, but persevere until it becomes more obvious again, skirting the summit of Skythorn Hill on the left, crossing over an old metal stile in a fence, then heading downhill towards Upper Glendevon Reservoir. Follow an obvious track and stay high until you emerge on a metalled road, near the reservoir dam. The track divides a couple of times, but stick to a middle line. The true right of way meanders round the far side of the reservoir, but it's much easier to cross the dam. Cross a fence near a stand of forestry and take the path into Glen Bee. Keeping to the left of Kinpauch Hill, head towards Blackford, now visible ahead. Head downhill across rough ground, making for a Land Rover track that can be seen ahead. Follow this track and cross the A9 with great care to enter Blackford at its western end.

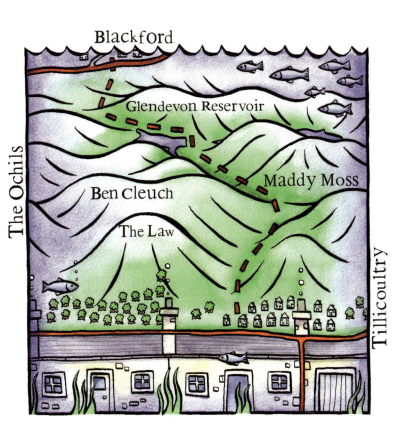

MAP	OS Sheet 58, Perth and Kinross
DISTANCE	10 miles (17km)
RATING	Strenuous. Hill paths and rough moorland
GEAR	Full hill-walking kit

THE AONACH EAGACH RIDGE

For adventurous souls with no fear of heights and a penchant for something more than a straightforward walk, a day tackling the Aonach Eagach is just the ticket.

THEMES Scotland's mountains resonate with the names of some of the most notable – and often notorious – names in climbing history. Tom Patey, Robin Smith, Hamish MacInnes, Chris Bonington, they are all there. The cliffs, corries and ridges of Ben Nevis, the Cairngorms and Glencoe have provided a stern testing ground for many who have aspired to feats in the Alps and the world's greater ranges. But those with more modest ambitions who still enjoy a frisson of excitement can tackle the sharper ridges without technical climbing experience. One of the most notable is the Aonach Eagach above Glencoe. Intimidating for anyone with no liking for steep drops, this serrated switchback is a challenge to anyone who relishes scrambling and has no fear of heights. Care is needed of course, but the ridge provides a superb day's outing with the bonus of a pub – the Clachaig Inn – right on the doorstep at the end of the day's exertions. The route is usually done from east to west, ending at the Clachaig, and two cars are required to avoid an unwelcome walk back up the glen.

ROUTE To start the day, park near the white cottage of Allt-na-reigh, just as the jaws of Glencoe are entered on the A82, after crossing Rannoch Moor. Follow the path which climbs up from the roadside to reach the south-east ridge of Am Bodach. There are two possible ascent routes. The more obvious goes directly up the ridge over steep, rocky ground, though there is a path to follow. Otherwise head along the path over the south-east ridge and in to the corrie on its eastern side, approaching Am Bodach from the rear. The path continues up the side of a burn, eventually reaching the summit. Am Bodach poses the first obstacle on the traverse with a scramble down polished rock, but on good holds. Then it's a question of following your nose along the winding ridge in airy situations. Further scrambling is required, particularly on the exposed Pinnacles section following the first of two Munros on the traverse, Meall Dearg. Then it's on to the second Munro, Sgorr nam Fiannaidh. You can descend to the south of this summit, avoiding the badly eroded and rather scary descent alongside Clachaig Gully. Alternatively, continue towards the Pap of Glencoe to descend easier ground on the left.

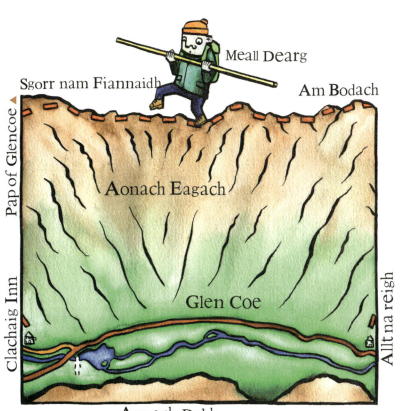

Meall Dearg

Sgorr nam Fiannaidh

Am Bodach

Pap of Glencoe

Aonach Eagach

Clachaig Inn

Glen Coe

Allt na reigh

Aonach Dubh

MAP	OS Sheet 41, Ben Nevis
DISTANCE	4 miles (6 km)
RATING	Strenuous. Undulating ridge with scrambling
GEAR	Full hill-walking kit

50

TENTSMUIR

They are the epitome of marine couch potatoes. Lazing on the sand bars off shore, or bobbing their heads out of the water, Tentsmuir's grey seals have an undeniable charm.

THEMES If you time your visit to be on the beach as the tide comes in, the seals get forced into the water off their sand bars and will venture close to shore. Scottish Natural Heritage manages the reserve and is justly proud of it, while the Forestry Commission is responsible for the woodland, covering about 4,000 acres of north-east Fife. Planted mostly with Scots and Corsican pine, the forest is a wildlife paradise and there are lots of birds to spot, as well as red squirrels and roe deer if you're fortunate. The name Tentsmuir derives from bygone days when fishermen pitched their tents on the dunes. A focal point in the forest is an abandoned ice house, once used for storing salmon, and kept cold with ice harvested from a nearby pond. These days the ice house is inhabited by bats, which have also been encouraged to roost in numerous bat boxes fixed to the trees.

ROUTE Start from the car park at Kinshaldy, reached by going through Leuchars. Take a right turn by a church, then further on a second right at a signpost. The road leads to the car park, where a small charge is levied. From the rear of the car park walk towards the beach and look for a green signpost with a yellow boot imprint on it. The path leads north in a straight line. It continues through the open pinewood to where another marker post points left on to a narrower, meandering section of path. Carry on along this to reach a wide forest track and turn right. Walk on to the ice house, where there are picnic tables. A short way east, past the ice house, is an entrance to Tentsmuir Nature Reserve with information signboards. Have a look at these, then return to the forest track. Turn north, heading for the edge of the forest. This is reached where the track bends round to the left and a tall wooden fingerpost marks the millennium cycleway and the Fife Coastal Path. Cross a stile on the right giving access to Tentsmuir Point. After the stile, turn immediately right to cross another stile over a fence. Walk down on to the beach and head south along the sand. Using the forest as a guide, walk on, curving gently round to the right, cutting across the widest part of the headland to regain the beach on the other side. Carry on to a fence, then turn right, back in towards the forest, to meet a nature reserve sign. Look for a yellow boot signpost and follow the marked path back to the car park.

Tentsmuir Point

Tentsmuir Forest

Leuchars

Tentsmuir Sands

MAP	OS Sheet 59, St Andrews
DISTANCE	6 miles (10 km)
RATING	Easy. Forest paths, tracks and sandy beach
GEAR	Boots and waterproof

51

THE BIRKS OF ABERFELDY

National Bard Robert Burns was a lover of the outdoors as well as the lassies, and this walk derives its name from one of his songs.

THEMES Although Burns is associated principally with his home ground in the farming communities of Ayrshire, Dumfries and Galloway, he did a fair bit of wandering about. In this case, a corner of the Perthshire town of Aberfeldy caught his attention.
So moved was he by the scenery that after a visit in August 1787 he wrote a song about it, with the opening verse containing the lines: "Bonnie lassie will ye go to the Birks of Aberfeldy?" With such a prominent connection to the Bard, it was inevitable that this walk would command attention. Following the tumbling Moness Burn – "the crystal streamlet" in the song – it climbs steeply upward before crossing a bridge and returning down the opposite side of the gorge through which the burn flows.

ROUTE Start from The Square in Aberfeldy and walk west along the main street. Turn left, following the blue sign to the Birks. Cross the Moness Burn at Craignish Bridge and carry on beside the burn. Ascend some steps and exit on the Crieff road at a gate. Cross the road and walk up the track to a car park. Go through it and turn left where the path divides, following the sign to Moness Falls. The path begins to climb in earnest, with bridges crossing small streams. Continue up more steps to Burns' Seat, where the poet is said to have rested and gained inspiration for his song. Steps lead up beside a waterslide and the path crosses the burn above it, with falls on the left. A long wooden bridge comes next, then a short path down to a viewing platform for the main falls. Return to the main path and up more steps. The route zig-zags upward to a bridge over the falls. There's another short climb before a much easier descent, with views of Strathtay and the surrounding hills. Back at the car park take the tree trail, which passes unusual exotic species such as Kashmiri whitebeam and Chinese scarlet rowan. Follow the road to the town centre and continue to the shapely Wade Bridge crossing the Tay – opened in October 1733 after frustrating delays. It was built at a cost of £3,596 – about £1m in today's money. There's also a memorial to the Black Watch regiment here. Finally, facing the Tay, turn right and follow the Moness Burn back to the town centre, passing the mill on the way.

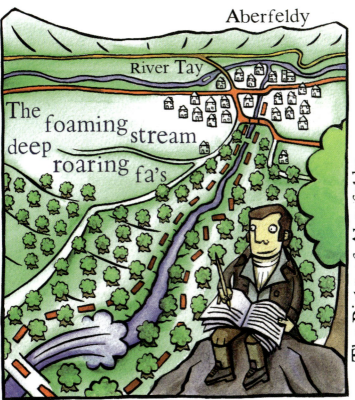

Aberfeldy

River Tay

The foaming stream
deep roaring fa's

The Birks of Aberfeldy

Falls of Moness

MAP	OS Sheet 52, Pitlochry to Crieff
DISTANCE	4 miles (6km)
RATING	Moderate. Waymarked paths can be muddy in places
GEAR	Boots and a waterproof

52

SKYE'S EASTERN RED HILLS

She must have been a formidable lady, the legendary Nordic princess known as Saucy Mary. Wife of a MacKinnon clan chief, she supposedly policed the Kyle of Lochalsh, levying tolls on ships that passed through.

THEMES Norwegian vessels going through the Kyle were exempt from Mary's toll and she reputedly gave them a flash of her bare breasts as they went by. On the rest she enforced the levy by means of a chain strung across the water. It was raised or lowered accordingly – though how quite Mary could have done this is a bit of a puzzle. She is said to be buried beneath the cairn on Beinn na Caillich, highest of the group of Skye's eastern red hills near Broadford. For a surprise, turn our illustration upside down. Another group lies to the west of these above Loch Sligachan, dominated by Glamaig – highest of all the reds. In 1899 a Gurkha soldier named Harkabir Thapa reached the summit of Glamaig, 2,542ft high, in an incredible 37 minutes, and returned in only 18. The red hills derive their name from the distinctive granophyte rock of which they are composed. In certain light conditions this takes on a pinkish tinge, differing markedly from the black gabbro of the main Cuillin ridge. Beinn na Caillich, whose Gaelic name means old woman, bears the distinction of being the first ever Skye peak to get a recorded ascent – by that well

known wanderer Thomas Pennant in 1772 from the MacKinnon household at Coire-chat-achan, the starting point of our walk, and now derelict.

ROUTE To follow in Pennant's footsteps and make your acquaintance with Saucy Mary, take the A881 out of Broadford towards Torrin, through Strath Suardal. In just over a mile there's a kink in the road at a chambered cairn, shown on the map. Just after the bend a path runs north to Coire-chat-achan, corrie of the wild cats. Walk west, climbing the shoulder of the hill. The steep heather slope gives way to boulders and then the grassy summit, with its huge cairn. With Coire Gorm below on your left, head round to the next hill, Beinn Dearg Mhor, or big red hill. A bealach is reached before the ascent to the top and another large cairn. From here there's a good view of the massive eastern ramparts of Cuillin outlier Blaven and its satellite Clach Glas. Carry on round the corrie over grass and scree down to Bealach Coire Sgreamhach and up to the top of little red hill – Beinn Dearg Beag. Continue on round and down the east ridge to Allt Beinn Deirge burn, which is followed back to the ruins of Coire-chat-achan and the path to the road.

Beinn na Caillich

Saucy Mary

Old Woman

Torrin A881

Broadford

MAP	OS Outdoor Leisure, Cuillin & Torridon Hills
DISTANCE	6.5 miles (11 km)
RATING	Moderate. Rough hill paths
GEAR	Full hill-walking kit

BIOGRAPHIES

PETER EVANS

Peter Evans moved to Scotland from his native South Wales more than 20 years ago. He is a former editor of *The Great Outdoors* magazine for walkers and *Climber* magazine, and has walked and climbed across Scotland in all seasons. Presently a production journalist with *Scotland on Sunday*, he is also a passionate advocate for the environment and has written many articles on subjects in that field of journalism. Together with his wife and two daughters, Peter lives in the Clackmannanshire town of Dollar, under the Ochils.

GLEN McBETH

Glen McBeth has been working as a freelance illustrator for over ten years. His distinctive and highly original work has appeared in magazines and newspapers around the world and has featured in various design and advertising projects. Glen's map illustrations began with the Walk of the Week feature in *Scotland on Sunday*. His maps aim to show a representation of the terrain and the colourful folklore and stories associated with walks.
www.glenmcbeth.co.uk

WALKS
RATING
INDEX

ALPHABETICAL INDEX